Mend It Better

MEND IT BETTER

Kristin M. Roach

Storey Publishing

The mission of Storey Publishing is to serve our customers by
publishing practical information that encourages
personal independence in harmony with the environment.

Edited by Deborah Balmuth and Nancy D. Wood
Art direction and book design by Alethea Morrison
Text production by Liseann Karandisecky

Cover photography by Greg Nesbit Photography except back
    cover top center by © Leah Peterson and front cover by
    Mars Vilaubi
Interior photography by Greg Nesbit Photography except
    for pages 79, 95, 102, 107, 117, 133, and 199 by ©
    Alexandra Grablewski; 15 bottom by © Evans/Three
    Lions/Getty Images; 144 by © Francesca Mueller; 5, 9,
    and 11 by © Kristin Roach; 64 by © Leah Peterson; 165
    and 186 by © Maja Blomqvist; 116 by © Marisa Lynch;
    58 and 73 by Mars Vilaubi; 14 and 15 middle by ©
    Mary Evans Picture Library/Alamy; 94 by © Stacie Wick;
    15 top and 16 left by © World History Archive/Alamy
Illustrations by © Kristin Nicholas

Indexed by Nancy D. Wood

The information in this book is true and complete to
the best of our knowledge. All recommendations are made
without guarantee on the part of the author or Storey
Publishing. The author and publisher disclaim any liability
in connection with the use of this information.

Storey books are available for special premium and
promotional uses and for customized editions. For further
information, please call 1-800-793-9396.

Storey Publishing
210 MASS MoCA Way
North Adams, MA 01247
www.storey.com

Printed in China by Toppan Leefung Printing Ltd.
10 9 8 7 6 5 4 3 2 1

Library of Congress Cataloging-in-Publication Data

Roach, Kristin M.
 Mend it better / Kristin M. Roach.
    p. cm.
 Includes index.
 ISBN 978-1-60342-564-3 (hardback)
 1. Clothing and dress—Repairing. I. Title.
TT720.R63 2012
646.2—dc23
                                    2011025032

To my grandma,

Phyllis Powell, whose memories fill me each
and every time I approach a sewing machine
or riffle through the fabric bin.

Contents

Introduction

*A*s I write this book, I keep my sister in mind. She is an amazing woman and I love her perspective on making things — she calls knitting "alchemy" and sewing "magic." Every time I bring a crochet project to a holiday gathering, she smiles with excitement as I turn my yarn into a scarf. I know she is capable of these arts, but I've never been able to empower her. While she has dabbled in stitching on buttons and shortening her pants (we Roach ladies are a short breed; I am the tallest at a towering 5' 3"), she has never felt confident enough to try to fix the broken zipper on her favorite purse, or take in the side seams of a cute jacket that is just a little too wide for her petite frame.

I am also writing this book for me, for my younger self, and for you. I am providing answers to all the questions I would have loved to have known back then, the techniques and tips that would have saved me countless hours of trial and error. My hope is that I'll be able to answer all those questions my younger self may have asked. With this book your and my sister's confidence will grow and you will all be filled with the desire and knowledge to make your wardrobe better.

Sewing skips a generation in my family. Not the skill of it, but the love for it. My Grandma Powell was a master seamstress on a miniature scale, though she sometimes made clothing for herself, my sister, and me, too. Her favorite thing was to spend time making elaborate Victorian clothes for the porcelain dolls that she would paint and fire in her basement. I grew up around piles of lace and doll-sized pantaloons. Sure, the usual amount of swearing went along with these projects, but she did love crafting and sewing. She even earned enough money selling her dolls to pay for a small kiln and a steady supply of materials for her craft. My Grandma Powell was the first crafty entrepreneur in my life.

My mom always suffered from the feeling that she just wasn't a creative person; she definitely didn't give herself enough credit. Looking back, I think that's one of the biggest fallacies of my childhood. She inspired and encouraged my sister and me in all kinds of crafty adventures. She may not have enjoyed it in quite the same way my grandma did, but she never let that stop her from painting little wood cutouts right along with us, crocheting an afghan for my favorite stuffed animals, or helping me sew my first dress. She was always brave and creative; no project was too hard to try. Even today, it might take her a while to admit to herself how inspiring she is, but my sister and I have known it for years.

As I was growing up, our neighbor was a constant inspiration as well. She showed us the benefit of trying new things and never stopped crafting with us kids. I spent countless hours drawing at her dining room table. And while my mom continued with yarn craft lessons, my neighbor, Deb, whom I have always considered my second mom, showed me the meditative nature of mending and handwork. She never sat me down and said, "Here is how you sew by hand and this is why it's so relaxing." It was the silent, contemplative way she went about it. Some of the sewing happened in her sewing room, a place of mystery and wonder. I would sneak in and look at all the buttons and run my hands over the piles of fabric. There she used the machine, but often she would bring her sewing up to the porch. Sipping tea, she would stitch away, with the wild excitement of her own four children (and plenty of us neighborhood kids adding to the chaos of it all) running around her. I am so happy that she accepted my offer to include one of her wonderful bags in this first book (see page 32).

It has been a long road from running around my grandma's sewing table to writing my own book. I went through a pretty punk phase of rejecting all things feminine when I was a teenager. Regrettably, during the years when I could have gained the most from my grandma's lifetime of sewing experience, I was not the least bit interested. Duct tape was the only mending tool I would go near and it covered just about everything: shoes, wallets, and heck, I even used it to fix the hem on my favorite skirt. I wanted to be a painter with a capital P and that left no time for women's work.

After my grandparents passed away, I was left with a void that was open and painful. I refused to let my grandma's sewing supplies be sold. My mom, seeing my pain, let me hold on to bins and bins of my grandma's fabric and yarn, her serger and sewing machine, and many of her crafting notions that I had no idea how to use. When I went away to college and had my own apartment, I slowly started to bring grandma's supplies home and taught myself how to use the tools of

My first two sewing machines were hand-me-downs from my grandma and great-aunt.

her trade. It was actually my partner, Jason, that encouraged me by teaching me how to knit my first stitches. Though my grandma didn't like to knit, she must have been bitten at some point by the knitting bug because among her stash of fabric and crochet hooks were scads of knitting needles, ranging in size from US 4 to 22.

Frequenting the local yarn shop became my favorite pastime, and it was not long before I started crocheting again. My first project was a teapot cozy that ended up looking like a cat-eared hat. I started digging more deeply into my grandma's stash, and quickly all of her sewing supplies found a home in my studio. I had done some very limited sewing in the years leading up to my time at university, but this was the first time that I made it up as I went along, and then committed instructions for those made-up items to paper.

My first sewing project was a canvas tote made out of leftover artist canvas from my painting class. This definitely made me take a closer look at which of the waste supplies from my painting courses could be used for other things.

....

More sewing, loads of knitting, a pile of crochet, and a few years later I was starting to carve out my career without even knowing it. I was just having fun sharing with others how I used up my leftover supplies.

....

When I first started Craft Leftovers (my website) in 2006, there was not much information online in the way of recycled craft patterns or specifics for using up your leftover bits. Now, just a few years later, I am excited that many others are on the same path as me, using what's on hand instead of running to the store, and inspiring others to do the same.

Mending has always been an important part of my Craft Leftovers website, because why go to the store or make more when you can repair? I started teaching mending workshops locally, so others could repair their own clothing. There was such a high demand for it. Before I knew it, I was getting requests and referrals to mend others' clothing, because they did not have the time or the know-how to do it themselves. I continued to delve further into mending in the following year and explored not just contemporary techniques, but old ones collected from vintage magazines. The local university has a huge collection of home economic literature dating back to the 1800s, amazingly fun to dig through.

Google Books has been another great source for finding so many wonderful writings that are now in the public domain. I discovered gems like "When Mother Lets Us Sew" and curriculum guides for girls in grades K to 8. When Storey Publishing contacted me about doing a mending book, I felt like everything came together. While they may not have known it (heck, I didn't even realize it), I had been preparing myself to write this book for the past three years of mending workshops, redress projects, and pattern writing.

I am so happy to be putting together this book and sharing what I have learned about mending. It is the next piece of my puzzle, to empower others to do their own mending. I am excited to bring to you not just my own mending experiences, but the experiences of over a dozen talented makers. Be inspired by their projects and stories, as well as my own. Mending can be technical, but it can also bring new life to old clothing. A creative bit of stitching and reshaping can make a dress that was banished to the back of the closet shine again. You can read this entire book and learn about all the facets of mending. Gathering advice from vintage magazines, old schoolbooks, my neighbor growing up, and my own trial and error, I have included all the information and instructions you need to repair your clothing and the clothing of those you love.

If you don't want to read this book from cover to cover, you can go straight to the subject that you need. Maybe this book caught your eye because of those pants at home that need a new zipper. Skip ahead to the section on zippers to learn how to fix or replace many different types of zippers. My hope is that through your mending successes, you will feel emboldened to express your creativity through your clothing. Start by adding trim or decorative stitching to a bland skirt, or maybe replace your old buttons with new fabric-covered ones that you've made yourself. Reject settling for a skirt with no pockets and add a cute patch pocket or maybe even a hidden inseam one.

Mending is a great form of sewing. While there are plenty of tools to be had, most sewing and almost all mending can easily be done with a minimal amount of supplies. Most of us already have one of those simple mending kits available in the checkout line of grocery stores. You can head home and get started right now. Mending is so accessible to everyone, and once you get the basics down you can share the skill with others, broadening this somewhat solitary activity into a social one. Mending can be simple or complex. It can be technical or creative. It saves money and preserves the favorite parts of your wardrobe. Sewing has existed long before cloth was ever woven, and along with sewing, came mending. Welcome to the practice of an ancient form of creative expression!

Kristin M Roach

The
Slim
Smooth
Smart
METAL
ZIPPER

A
Color
Keyed

HER SIDE

wing Guide Line
Stronger Chain
Precision Slider
Automatic Lock

Style 110

DONAHUE

Mending, Then and Now

〜◦〜

Let me take you on a short trip through time and show you how we have progressed from throwing around rocks to mass-producing ready-to-wear clothing. Then we'll talk about some of the common mending problems that you might come across today.

The Evolution of Sewing

This tale begins all the way back in ancient Egypt. Before people spun wool into yarn and wove yarn into cloth, they used animal hides and parts to protect themselves from the elements, show status in their communities, and make some pretty impressive tools. Single-blade scissors were found in ancient Egypt ruins, dated to 1500 BCE.

It's hard to think of a time when sewing did not exist, but the sewing needle, often made from bone, was quite the revolution. Spinning had not been invented yet, so thread was not available, but guts were. Sewing animal hides together with guts and hair? Gross, right? But you have to admit it's pretty resourceful and made quite the difference in day-to-day life. Things like shoes and animal-skin water sacks came into being.

Because of the nature of sewing leather with sharpened bones, the thimble came along in pretty short order. At first, thimbles were probably made from animal hides, but once iron and metal came into the picture, little metal thimbles started showing up in archaeological digs. The earliest known sewing kit, found in China, had several iron thimbles and needles in it. Around that same period, CE 100, Romans developed an innovation that we all still use today: the cross-blade scissors. It was not until the sixteenth century, though, that they came into common use in Europe.

Everything really started changing quickly in the late eighteenth century. England secured their lead in the textile manufacturing industry by passing a law forbidding the export of any drawings, written specifications, or machinery. They wanted to be the only ones to have power looms and the ability to spin yarn by mechanized means for as long as possible. What is a power loom and what made it so powerful? It was quite the breakthrough by Francis Cabot Lowell, and allowed, for the first time, the mechanical reproduction of loom weaving with steam power.

POWER LOOMS

THE SPINNING JENNY

THE COTTON GIN

THIMONNIER'S MACHINE

The spinning jenny was another machine that established England as industrial leaders. In the eighteenth century, James Hargreaves invented this device that was able to replace eight spinners with just one machine.

Textile manufacturing took another great leap in 1793, but this time from the other side of the ocean in the United States of America. Eli Whitney and Hogden Holmes invented the cotton gin. This machine provided a simple way to remove cotton lint from the seeds, a process that would normally take many hands to sort and pick the seeds apart. It helped push the textile industry a little closer toward mass-produced clothing.

All the processes of textile manufacturing were starting to become mechanized: cotton picking, spinning, and weaving. Then finally, the last step happened — machine sewing! Barthelemy Thimonnier caused quite the uproar in 1830 when he patented the first sewing machine and then set up a factory full of them. His idea was to mass-produce French army uniforms and make buckets of money. Unfortunately for Barthelemy, 200 local tailors rioted on the morning of January 20, 1831. They broke into the factory, ransacked the equipment, and threw the chain stitching machines out the windows. Rightly so, Barthelemy fled for his life. He never did see those buckets of money and lived out the rest of his life in near poverty.

In 1834, Walter Hunt designed a machine that made a backstitch that was stronger than the chain stitching method. Concerned about the effect that his machine would have on the local labor force (maybe even in fear of another riot), he opted not to patent it. However, he did go on to invent and patent one of my very favorite sewing notions — the safety pin! What would we do without them? Thanks, Walt!

The development of sewing machines marched on despite labor unease. It was Elias Howe, in September 1846, who patented the lockstitch sewing machine. It was the first practical sewing machine built to date. The key word here is "practical." Up until then, there had been many attempts, but none of the new machines were very useful in an industrial application.

Howe started developing a sewing machine after being told by Ari Davis, a precision machinist, that a practical sewing machine would make a man rich. From that point on, Howe spent every spare hour working on this machine. His success came when he chose

to think outside the box. Instead of trying to reproduce hand stitches like so many before him, he employed his knowledge of established machine techniques to build the first lockstitch sewing machine. It had a needle with a hole in the end and used two threads that interlocked at a speed of about 250 stitches per minute, out-stitching the work of five humans. And, it was very expensive at $300, which is around $8,000 in contemporary currency. Though sales were bad, Howe did eventually make it rich through patent lawsuits and royalty payments. Just about every sewing machine built since then is a modification of the basic components of his original.

In the 1850s, A. B. Wilson added his special contribution to the modern sewing machine: feed dogs and bobbins. Before his enhancements, fabric was fed by way of a belt with spikes on it.

HOWE'S LOCKSTITCH SEWING MACHINE

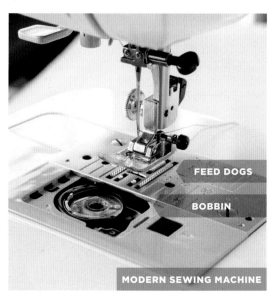

FEED DOGS

BOBBIN

MODERN SEWING MACHINE

Singer has always been a big name in sewing. My first two sewing machines were Singers, one passed down from my great-aunt and the other from my grandma. Did you know that it was Isaac Merritt Singer who brought us the foot treadle and easier handling of the fabric with the presser foot? For the first time, sewers could use both hands to maneuver the fabric through the machine. Singer, oh, what an innovator he was! He also designed the current position of the needle. In early machines, the needle moved from side to side. His machine utilized and perfected the vertical sewing needle.

The designers and inventors I have mentioned were just the main players in the development of our modern sewing machine. Many others made contributions along the way. All of the sewing machine innovations changed the work of the homemaker. Up to this point, making an article of clothing by hand took about 14 hours. With the use of the sewing machine, like the ones being sold in the Sears catalogs as early as 1897, the same project might take only two hours. This left women with time to do fun things, like fight for the right to vote!

There were some inevitable downsides to the growing trend of mass-produced clothing. Before long, women's groups were lamenting the loss of the domestic arts, which were instead being performed by machines in factories. To make ends meet, many women and girls ended up working in the textile factories instead of taking work home. This is when the study of home economics in the schools came into existence. The women of Boston developed the first school curriculum that taught basic sewing skills to girls, since girls were no longer learning domestic arts at home. While it may seem a completely strange concept now, girls were expected to know these skills to be a good wife and mother. Another inevitable change was the availability and affordability of ready-to-wear clothing. Originally, all clothing was handmade, tailored to fit each person. It was time-consuming to make clothing and expensive to hire someone else do it. Most people only had a few articles of clothing, maybe a new shirt or two each year. As the looms wove the cloth and the sewing machines stitched away, clothing became more accessible — a great thing really.

When locomotives, planes, trains, and boats became more common, they pushed the manufacture and sale of textiles and clothing forward, the final chapter of the textile revolution. So now, not only was clothing quicker to make, it was cheaper, too. All of this led to the manufacture of clothing that has become seemingly disposable in nature. Instead of letting the clothes you love filter down into the landfill, let me show you how to extend their life almost indefinitely.

While mending and general sewing are no longer required skills, they are still very helpful skills to know. Mending is also a great way to start sewing because it's relatively easy. It's very useful in extending the life of the garments you love and saving you a bit of money. As a bonus, the successful completion of most projects will reward you with instant gratification. So, let's get stitching. That's why we are here, right?

To Mend or Not to Mend

W̸hile I'm a firm believer in the principle of "waste not, want not," even I must face the fact that some clothing is best retired to the scrap pile. Every time I approach a mending project, I consider the following key questions before I commit it to my mending bag.

Do I love it?

This is a big one, and I think the most important question. Why take the time to fix a shirt that you don't really care for?

Will someone else love it?

Sometimes I'll fix an item I don't like if it's something I know a friend will like. Or, if it's a sturdy piece that just needs a button or something simple like that, I'll fix it and donate it to the local Salvation Army.

How much time, money, and skill will it take?

Different projects take different skills. Some projects will, by their nature, take more time to mend than others. And some projects will take money if you need to replace buttons, snaps, zippers, or even buy specialized tools like eyelet pliers. Take into consideration the time and money it will take to complete your mending project, the uniqueness of the item, the material it is made out of, and how much you love it.

The love-it factor is one I'll repeat over and over because it really is the most important consideration. I have a messenger bag that cost only $20. I bought it from a clothing boutique in Iowa City when I was just 17 years old and I love it to this day. When it started falling apart, I ignored it at first, and when I finally sat down to mend it, it took quite the time and monetary investment to get it back into working order. There was no question in my mind whether or not to spend the time and money needed to save it. Not only is it a really neat bag, but it also has a lot of sentimental value.

Is it a junk item?

Unfortunately a lot of clothes are made to be disposable. The seams rip, the threads go bare, the buttons fall off. If you love it (the first question), go for it. If you don't, you might put it to better use as a rag to mop up the floor.

Is the fabric high quality?

If so, definitely give mending a try before retiring it.

Is the rest of the garment in good condition?

This is part of the time commitment question, really. If you fix the button, will you need to patch a hole or fix a zipper, too? Give the whole garment a once-over before you decide whether or not to mend it.

Is the area to be mended stretched or distorted? Frayed?

This will make any mending project infinitely more complex and annoying.

Is the fabric easy to work with?

Time and frustration are major factors for me when considering which projects to work on. Consider the fabric before jumping in. Slippery fabrics, lace, stretch, and some patterned fabrics are not the easiest to sew or mend.

I once had a pair of jeans that I bought for $8. I loved them. So when the seams started tearing, I fixed them. When the fabric started wearing thin after just a few washes, I reinforced it. Those jeans could have been retired after just a few months, but because I loved them so much I opted to take the time to fix them, even though they were pretty much disposable.

Every time you approach a mending project, the solution will be different. It all depends on the fabric type, the color of the garment, and the scope of the damage. Learning the best way to repair your clothes will keep them in working order longer than just whipping some stitches over the tear. Oh, consider that phrase we have all heard a million times: "Take the time to do it right the first time and you will save time in the long run."

How hard is it to fix?

If you are mending for the first time, you might want to start out with some of the basic techniques, like sewing on a button or fixing a hem. If you have a lot of sewing under your belt, or are the adventurous "I can do anything" type, like I am, definitely dive right in with replacing a zipper or fixing a tear in your favorite leather coat. At right is a list, organized by difficulty, of some of the most common mending adventures.

HELPFUL HINTS FOR MENDING

WORK IN A WELL-LIT AREA. This will help you see your work clearly, relieve eyestrain, and make mending an easier task.

KEEP YOUR MENDING KIT STOCKED AND TIDY. A messy collection of supplies slows down a mending project quicker than any amount of tedious hand sewing. How can you mend if you can't find your scissors? (See page 37 for instructions on making a very useful mending clutch.)

KEEP YOUR HANDS CLEAN. Nothing is worse than carefully mending your favorite shirt, only to realize that you have gotten drawing charcoal all over it. Switching from drawing to mending can be tricky business. Wash your hands before you get started!

RAISE YOUR WORK INSTEAD OF BENDING YOUR BACK. Mending can be uncomfortable if you are crowding over your work. To avoid neck and back pain, lift your work in front of you, so you are not hunched. I like to work on mending at my kitchen table to keep myself from bending at odd angles.

MEND FIRST, WASH AFTER. It's often the case that the clothing you will be repairing is dirty. It's when we are out and about that buttons usually fall off, seams tear, and snags snag — not when the clothing is folded neatly in the dresser. To keep the item from being further damaged, mend it before washing it in the washer.

PRESS FIRST, MEND AFTER. Just like any sewing project, it's best to press the area you are stitching before you get started. Without pressing, it's harder to make straight lines, match up buttons to buttonholes, and patch tears without bunching the fabric. Just press it, and then mend it. It will look much nicer in the end.

EASY FIXES

- Working on heavyweight fabric that's patterned and textured
- Shortening and restitching a hem
- Patching clothes when you don't mind seeing the history of mending
- Restitching any ripped seam
- Sewing a button back on
- Darning a single snag
- Restringing a drawstring
- Replacing elastic in a casing
- Repairing topstitching
- Fixing or shortening buttonholes
- Repairing or patching an in-seam pocket

INTERMEDIATE FIXES

- Working on woven fabrics like broadcloth and denim, single knits, machine-made lace, and solid color fabrics
- Adding length to a hem
- Darning a hole
- Replacing elastic that has been stitched on
- Repairing a ripped and completely frayed buttonhole
- Fixing darts
- Changing a garment's shape

ADVANCED FIXES

- Working on specialty fabrics like lace, satin, and silk
- Mending anything that is in a highly visible location
- Replacing a buttonhole that's been torn out completely
- Replacing a broken zipper
- Relining a whole garment
- Removing press marks and stains

Mending Tool Kit

The best thing about mending is that you more than likely have everything you need to fix or repurpose your torn and tired clothing in your home. Gather the right tools and create your own little mending kit.

What You Need

*O*ne of the great things about mending is its accessibility. All you really need is a needle and thread and scissors. Of course there are many great tools for mending, but when you are just starting out or you're on the go, you don't need to look any further than the basics. Over time, you may want to expand your selection of mending tools to include more specialized items. You don't need to run out and buy them all at once, but you'll want to get them as you need them, depending on the mending projects you tackle.

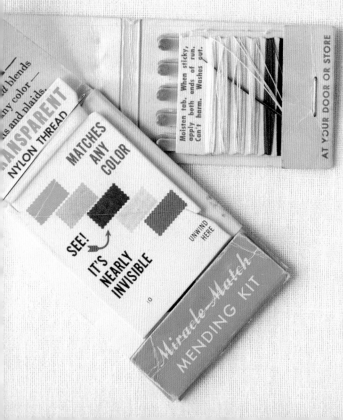

BASIC MENDING SUPPLY KIT

➼ Assortment of hand-sewing needles

➼ Black, white, and gray cotton-covered polyester thread

➼ Small scissors

➼ Seam ripper

➼ Iron and ironing board

➼ Fabric marking pen or chalk

➼ Seam gauge or ruler

➼ Several straight pins and safety pins

Keeping Things in Place

Ⓐ DRESSMAKER PINS: 1⅙" all-purpose pins for keeping things in place while working your mending magic.

Ⓑ SAFETY PINS: my favorite mending tool; perfect for holding temporary fixes, pinning patches in place, and marking where buttons should go.

Ⓒ T-PINS: great for heavy and open-weave fabrics; the bar of the T keeps the pin from slipping right though the fabric.

For Hand Sewing

Ⓓ SHARPS: these needles are for all-purpose hand sewing; they're short, sharp, and have a hole (eye) just the right size for thread.

Ⓔ EMBROIDERY: this little needle has an eye large enough for embroidery floss and thinner yarns; it's good for basic darning needs and decorative stitching.

Ⓕ DARNING: for more serious darning operations, it's nice to have this long needle with a long eye in your stitching arsenal.

Ⓖ THIMBLE: a hand-sewing accessory to protect your finger (see page 46).

For Machine Stitching

Ⓗ STANDARD/UNIVERSAL: all of your general stitching needs are taken care of by these beauties; keep extra around at all times, in a variety of sizes.

Ⓘ BALL POINT: a little more specialized, but great to have on hand; use them on knit and other stretch fabrics.

Ⓙ JEANS: a heavy-duty needle; sharp, thick, and just the trick for pushing through layers of denim and other heavyweight fabrics.

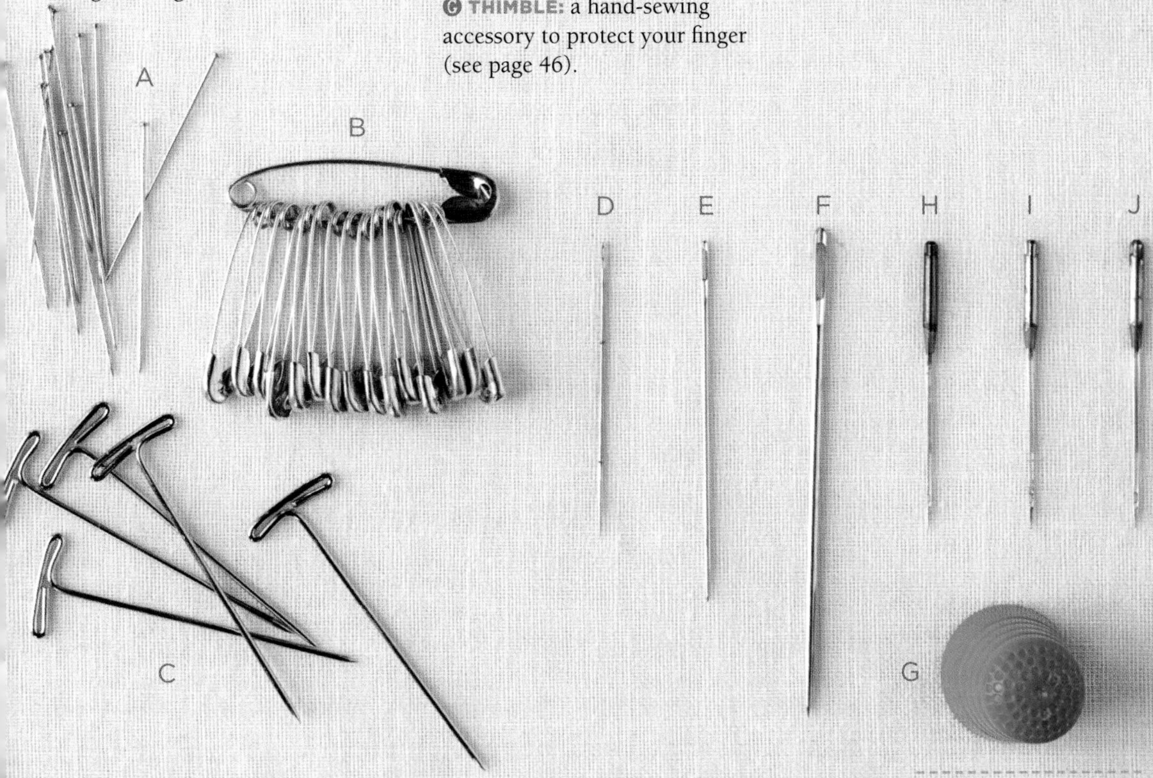

A

B

C

D   E   F   H   I   J

G

This apron of Eirlys Penn, a.k.a. Scrapiana, shows the signs of a well-worn favorite. To mend the frayed edges in an understated way that doesn't change the apron's basic feel, Eiryls is using ordinary white herringbone-weave cotton tape, folded around the edges and secured with a stab stitch, often used to bind the edges of a quilt.

For Measuring

I cannot tell you how often I wished I had measured out my work before even thinking of touching my scissors. Take the time to measure your seam allowances, your own self, and your hems, and you will save so much time and frustration.

Ⓐ TRANSPARENT RULER: helpful for marking straight lines.

Ⓑ TAILOR'S TAPE MEASURE: small, compact, and great for using any time the body is involved; you can measure yourself, measure fabric, or measure seams, and because of its flexibility you can even measure on a curve.

Ⓒ SEAM GAUGE: the handiest ruler you can have in your mending tool kit; it doubles as a ruler for general measuring and a gauge to mark hems.

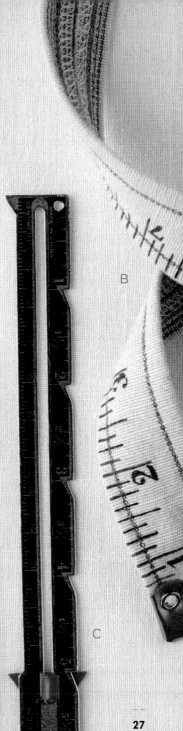

B

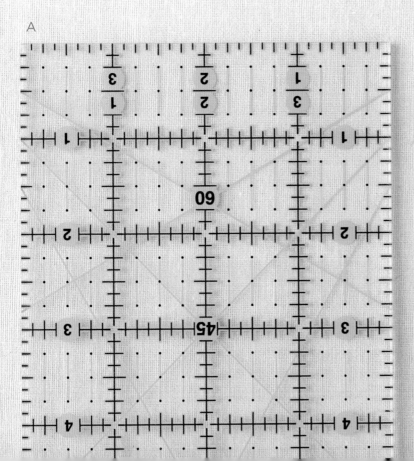

A

C

For Cutting

Using the optimal cutting tool for the job will give you the best possible mending results. The whole idea is that you don't need a jackhammer to pull out a nail.

A SEAM RIPPER: you often have to rip out a few extra stitches from a torn seam before you can fix it correctly, or if you botch anything, a seam ripper is your best friend for making things right again.

B EMBROIDERY SCISSORS: pointed scissors that can double for general scissors and/or a seam ripper; I keep a pair in my on-the-go mending kit and my home kit. My grandma attached a pair (the classic ones that look like a crane) to her needle book with a ribbon, so they would always be ready for trimming thread and snipping bits of this and that.

C SEWING SCISSORS: slightly smaller than shears, about 6" long, they are great for cutting patches, trimming seams, and cleaning up holes for patching. One point is sharp and the other is rounded and blunt.

D PINKING SHEARS: definitely not a "must have" item, but very handy, especially if you have yet to acquire a serger; use them to trim raw edges to prevent fraying.

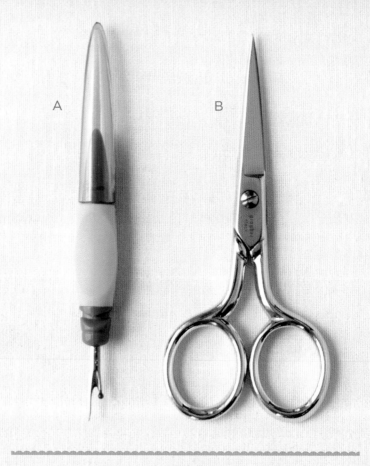

PROTECTING SCISSORS

Everyone knows not to touch my sewing scissors. If they want to cut paper or anything that's not fabric, they know better than to even ask to use my scissors with the pink handles. Why am I so particular about them? Well, using your super-sharp fabric scissors on paper will dull them, and dull scissors chew through fabric and shred thread, making for a very obnoxious mending time. I bought the most ridiculous pink-handled scissors to make them distinctly different from all our other pairs. If your fabric scissors are the same color as your paper scissors, tie a piece of fabric around one of the handles. It's like a little flag of warning not to touch your good scissors.

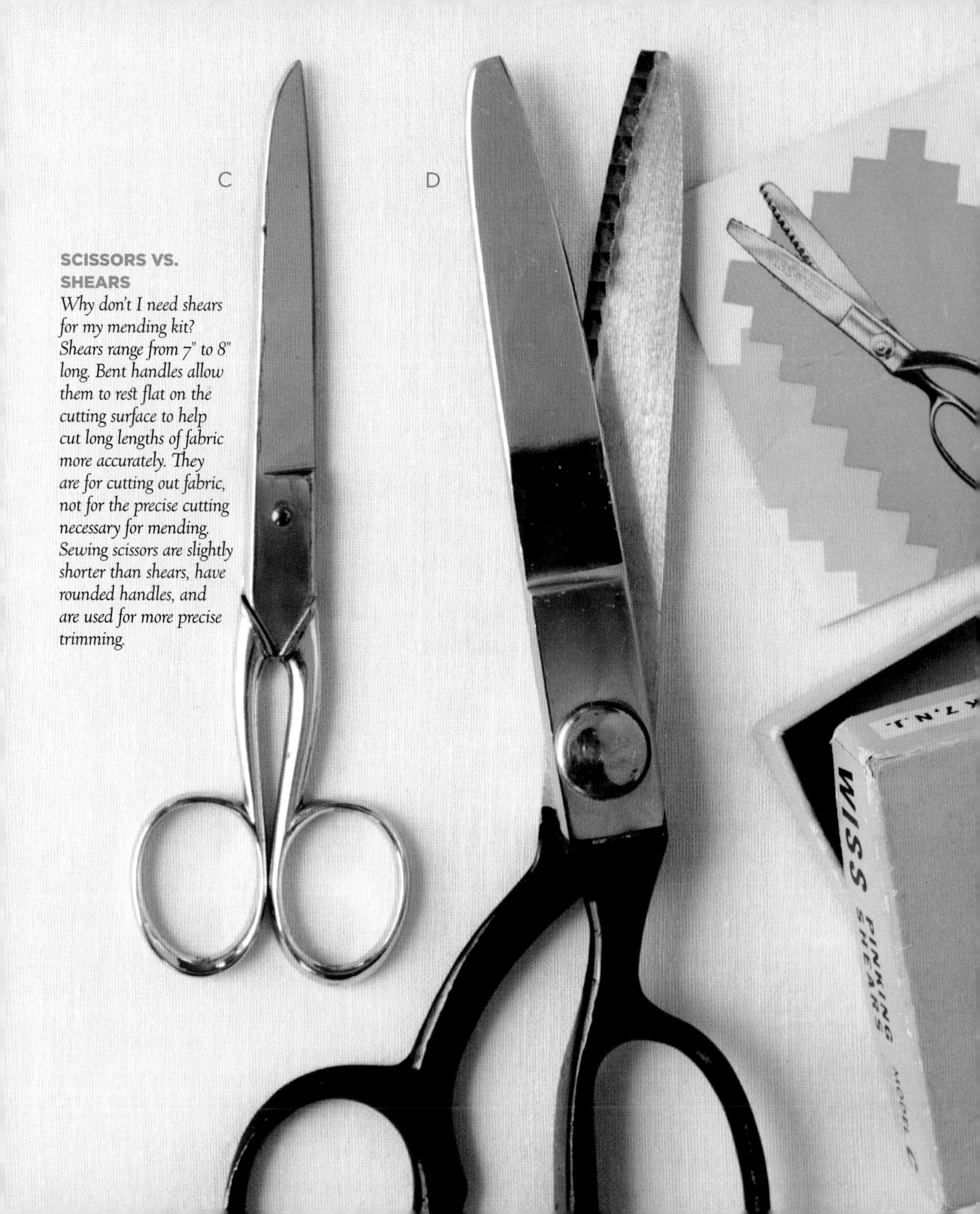

C   D

SCISSORS VS. SHEARS

Why don't I need shears for my mending kit? Shears range from 7" to 8" long. Bent handles allow them to rest flat on the cutting surface to help cut long lengths of fabric more accurately. They are for cutting out fabric, not for the precise cutting necessary for mending. Sewing scissors are slightly shorter than shears, have rounded handles, and are used for more precise trimming.

WISS

PINKING SHEARS

MODEL C

N. J.

For Marking

Sometimes it's necessary to mark the fabric with the design that you plan to cut or want to stitch. Here are some tools that can help you with that.

Ⓐ SOAP SLIVERS: My favorite marking tool; if the soap doesn't have a fine enough edge, you can use a paring knife to sharpen it.

Ⓑ CHALK: Nope, not sidewalk chalk. There are many types of chalk you can get from the sewing shop. There are pencils with chalk instead of lead, rolling chalk dispensers, and chalk wedges (I like these). You can use blackboard chalk in a pinch, but the colors may leave residual pigment in your fabric, so beware.

Ⓒ TRACING WHEELS AND PAPER: A great way to transfer a design or pattern markings onto paper or fabric is with a tracing wheel and tracing paper. Position the tracing paper with the colored side down on the paper or fabric, with the pattern or design you want to copy on top. Then run the wheel along the pattern lines. The wheel makes marks that look like a line on the paper or fabric. If you are going to transfer the marks directly onto your fabric, be sure to test it first to make sure the transferred marks come off and don't harm the fabric.

Ⓓ FABRIC-MARKING PENS AND PENCILS: *Washable* and *fade-away* are the two main types of fabric marking pens and pencils. The washable type will stay on your fabric until you wash it. The other will fade over time; the amount of time it takes to fade depends on the type of pencil. Make sure to mark just before you cut or sew, because the marks are likely to fade if you don't start sewing right away.

Thread Know-How

The kind of thread you use for your project really does make a difference. Here are the most common threads you will need for your mending projects.

Ⓐ POLYESTER THREAD: good for synthetic blend and stretch fabrics because it has some stretch and doesn't shrink.

Ⓑ COTTON THREAD: has less give then its synthetic counterparts; best used on wool, linen, and cotton fabrics, works very well with woven fabrics.

Ⓒ COTTON-WRAPPED POLYESTER THREAD: a great all-purpose thread that can be used on synthetics and natural fiber fabrics.

Ⓓ TOPSTITCHING THREAD: also called *utility* or *dual duty* thread, topstitching thread is little thicker and stronger than most. It works perfectly for topstitching, but is also the best choice for sewing on buttons, making buttonholes, and attaching any other type of fastener.

Ⓔ EMBROIDERY FLOSS: a mercerized cotton or soft silk thread used in embroidery and needlework. Usually a grouping of six to eight threads is worked as one, but the strands can be separated from each other to work finer stitching.

For Finishing

Ⓐ FRAY PREVENTION GLUE: while not completely necessary, this is a great quick-fix tool to have on hand right from the get-go.

Ⓑ IRON, IRONING BOARD, AND PRESSING CLOTH: (not pictured) a steam iron and sturdy ironing board is necessary for professional-looking results; a pressing cloth protects your fabric from the surface of a hot iron.

A   B   C   D

E

A

REPURPOSED MENDING BAG

by Deb Cory

I have had people apologize for the sorry state of a tablecloth, doily, or towel that they were offering for sale. I would smile sweetly, sure that they felt I was settling for damaged goods. If only they knew that I was chomping at the bit to take the article home, launder it, hang it on the line, examine all the spoiled spots, and plan its creative revival.

Make a rule for yourself, as you venture from thrift shop to yard sales, to never pass up a fine fabric just because it's not useful any longer for the purpose that it was intended. Good cloth is good cloth, and often its next life is more exciting than its original. This bag was made from an assortment of rejects: a 1950s tablecloth made from a strong cotton/linen fabric; an extravagantly embroidered linen table runner that was damaged in the middle; and a cast-off web belt with a nice lace embellishment.

What You'll Need

1 recycled tablecloth (or other fabric source), for the bag front and back

Large muslin or cotton scraps, for lining

Fusible fleece, enough to line the bag and possibly the pocket

1 recycled embroidered cloth, such as a table runner, for the pocket

Recycled fabric belt for straps

Mending supply kit (see page 24)

Sewing machine (optional)

What You'll Do

Step 1. Lay out the table-cloth and consider the most prudent way to utilize the whole piece. Do not waste. Perfectly recyclable table-cloths might not come around again. Decide on the desired size (height and width) of the mending bag. How much room do you need for your mending projects and supplies? You can look at other bags you like and measure them. If you have something specific that will work for the pocket, plan to make the bag at least 2" larger than the pocket on all sides.

Step 2. Draw two rectangles the desired width and length (adding ½" seam allowances all around) onto the tablecloth, with an eye for showcasing any fabric designs that you like. Keep in mind that the front of the bag will be covered with a large pocket. Cut out the rect-angles. While you're at it, cut two rectangles the same size from the lining fabric and two from the fusible fleece.

Step 3. Press the fleece (it will give body to the bag) to the wrong side of both outside bag pieces, following the manufacturer's instructions. You now have two interfaced panels, front and back.

Step 4. A well-loved table runner can make the perfect pocket for your bag. (This one was damaged in the center, so I cut off both embroidered ends. I used one for the pocket and set the other aside for another project.) Cut the pocket to fit the front of the bag, with ½" extra on all sides for seam allowances. My pocket is very large, but the size is up to you.

Step 5. If your pocket and lining fabrics are lightweight or limp, you might want to apply a piece of fusible fleece or heavyweight fusible interfacing on the wrong side of the lining and/or the pocket. If so, apply the fleece or interfacing at this stage, and then make and attach the pocket (see Making a Basic Lined Pocket on page 35).

Step 6. After the pocket is attached, pin the front and

back panels with the right sides together. Starting at the top edge, stitch down one side, across the bottom, and back up to the opposite top edge, pivoting at the corners and backstitching at both ends.

Step 7. To make corner gussets, align the bottom seam and the side seam on both sides of the bag. Finger-press the seam allowance to one side. The corner will form a point as illustrated below. Stitch an arc across the corner about 3" from the point, backstitching at each end of the seam. Repeat for the other corner and then set the outer bag aside.

Step 8. Pin the two lining pieces with right sides

together. Stitch from one top edge, down the side, around the bottom, and up the other side, backstitching at both ends. Create gussets for the liner as in step 7.

Step 9. Slip the lining into the outer bag with wrong sides together, to check the fit. Adjust as needed and remove the lining. Press under the top edges of the lining and the outer bag ½". Again slip the lining into the bag, matching the side seams and the top hemmed edges. Pin the top edges together, all the way around, but don't stitch yet.

Step 10. To make the straps, fold the belt in half and sling it over your shoulder. Get a good feel for the length you would

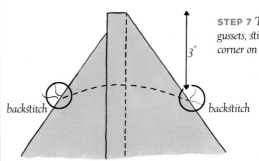

STEP 7 *To make corner gussets, stitch an arc across each corner on the inside of the bag.*

3"

backstitch

backstitch

like the handles to be, and cut the belt into two pieces, each the desired length. Insert the ends of each strap between the outer bag and the lining and pin them in place. The exact placement is up to you, but it's a good idea to measure from the side edge to each strap to make sure they are the same distance from the sides.

Step 11. Edgestitch around the top of the bag, backstitching across the four strap ends to add extra strength. Using a decorative stitch is a great option here.

MAKING A BASIC LINED POCKET

A lined pocket is very simple to make. You can use another piece of the pocket fabric as lining as long as it isn't too heavy or bulky. If the fabric is heavy, use lining fabric, or a remnant from your stash.

Step 1. Decide on the size and shape of the pocket and add ½" on all sides for the seam allowance.

Step 2. Cut a pocket front and a pocket lining to the desired measurements. If you have an unusually shaped pocket, it might help to make a paper pattern first and use it to cut the fabric.

Step 3. Pin the pocket front and lining with the right sides together, and stitch a ½" seam on all sides, leaving a 2" to 3" opening for turning.

Step 4. Clip away the seam allowance at the corners and turn the pocket right side out. Tuck the seam allowance evenly into the opening. You don't have to hand-sew the opening closed because stitching it to the bag (or other item) will close the opening.

Step 5. Pin the pocket in place on the project (in this case the Mending Bag) and edgestitch (see page 53) around the sides and bottom, pivoting at the corners and backstitching at both top edges to secure.

A large or wide pocket can be stitched down the middle (after it is applied to the item), to divide one pocket into two sections, making it perfect for holding pens and scissors, not to mention Kristin's Mending Tool Clutch (see page 37).

MAKING A LINED POCKET WITH TRIMMED VINTAGE FABRIC

The pocket shown on the bag on page 33 has a rounded bottom and lace trim. If you were to line the pocket as instructed on page 35, that lovely lace trim would disappear into the seam allowance. So if you're using existing fabric with trim already attached, here's an alternative method:

Step 1. Place the pocket front on top of the lining piece. Trace around the fabric edge of the pocket (not including the lace trim), then add an extra ½" on all sides for seam allowance.

Step 2. Cut out the pocket lining. Baste ½" from the edge around the curved sides only.

Step 3. Pin the top edge of the pocket front and lining with the right sides together. Stitch a ½" seam.

Step 4. Press the seam toward the lining, using the basting stitches as a guide.

Step 5. Press the remaining (curved) edges of the pocket lining ½" to the wrong side along basting line. Notch or overlap the seam allowance at the curves as needed.

Step 6. Pin the pocket front and lining with wrong sides together so the stitched seam is at the top and the lace extends beyond the edges of the lining. Edgestitch across the top of the pocket. To make the next step easier, baste the pocket to the lining around the open edges, removing pins as you stitch.

Step 7. Pin the pocket to the bag. Edgestitch the sides and bottom of the pocket, backstitching at both top edges.

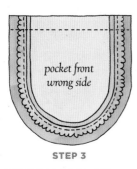

pocket front
wrong side

STEP 3

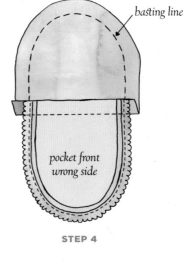

basting line

pocket front
wrong side

STEP 4

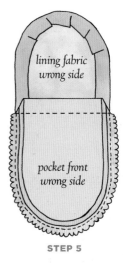

lining fabric
wrong side

pocket front
wrong side

STEP 5

MENDING TOOL CLUTCH

by Kristin Roach

Having this handy kit tucked into the front pocket of your mending bag will help you pull off all of your mending projects without a hitch. Keep this clutch sacred. Never take anything out of it to use for general sewing or before you know it, the clutch will be empty. You will spend your time looking for your mending tools instead of using them.

What You'll Need

Template for the clutch
(see page 41)

Scrap of felted sweater or heavy
wool felt for exterior

Lighter weight fabric scraps for
interior

12" of ¼"-wide elastic

1 polyester zipper, at least 7" long

1 metal zipper, at least 14" long

Mending supply kit (see page 24)

Sewing machine and zipper foot
(optional)

What You'll Do

Step 1. Enlarge the template
200%, or to desired size, and
use it to cut the following:

•➤ One piece the full size of
the template from the felted
sweater (exterior)

•➤ One piece the full size
of the template from fabric
(interior)

•➤ One A piece and one B
piece from fabric

Step 2. On the large interior fabric piece, lay out your
supplies (pins, thread, and
so forth) and plan where the

little pieces of elastic need to
go to hold them. To match the
placement pictured, follow
the illustration for the finished
interior layout. Cut some
scraps from the felted sweater
to use as pads for holding buttons and sticking safety pins.
Hand-sew the pieces of elastic
and pads of fabric in place. If
you're using a fabric other than
felt, work a blanket stitch (see
page 52) around the edges of
the pads so they don't fray.

Step 3. Switch the presser
foot on your machine to a
zipper foot (or sew by hand).
Make the interior zippered
pouch as follows:

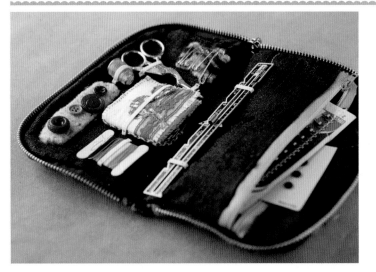

STOCKING THE CLUTCH

• Buttons
• Safety pins
• Embroidery scissors
• Seam gauge
• Scrap fabric and fusible webbing
  for making patches
• Sew-on snaps and hooks
• Thimble
• Thread in black, white, and gray
  wrapped around an embroidery
  floss card
• Needle book (to make your own,
  see page 54)

◆◆ Pin the closed 7" zipper to one long edge of piece A with the right sides together and stitch with a ⅛" seam allowance. Fold the zipper right side up and edgestitch on the fabric, close to the seam.

◆◆ Open the zipper and then pin the other side of the zipper to one long edge of piece B with the right sides together. Stitch, press, and edgestitch on right side as in the previous step.

◆◆ Switch back to a regular presser foot on your sewing machine. Press the other long edge of piece B ¼" to the wrong side.

◆◆ Place the large interior piece right side up. Position piece A/B on top of the interior piece (as shown), matching the curved edges and pin in place. Stitch close to the folded edge of piece B and then around all the sides of A/B to attach it to the large interior piece.

Step 4. Attach the 14" zipper to the exterior piece as follows:

◆◆ Lay the exterior piece right side up and fold it in half. Use a fabric marker to mark the center fold line. Unfold the fabric.

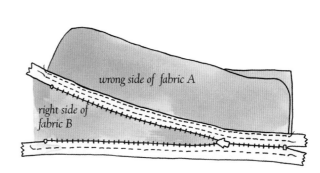

wrong side of fabric A

right side of fabric B

STEP 3 *attaching the interior zipper*

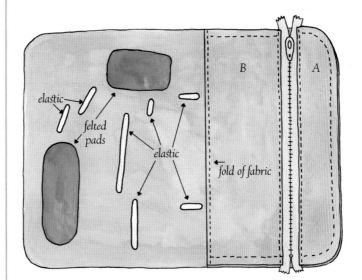

elastic

felted pads

elastic

B

A

fold of fabric

FINISHED INTERIOR LAYOUT

With the zipper closed, pin it with right sides together to the exterior piece, positioning the zipper head at the center fold line. Mark and pin the zipper tape around to the opposite fold line. The zipper will be longer than the exterior piece; extend the extra zipper tape inside the fabric piece.

Install the zipper foot on your sewing machine and sew the zipper in place, backstitching at the beginning and end of the seam.

With the zipper closed, fold the exterior piece in half and pin the other half of the zipper (starting at the end with the zipper head) to one short side and about half of the long side with the right sides together. Stitch, backstitching at the beginning of the seam and pivoting at the corner.

Open the zipper about 4", then pin the rest of the zipper to the exterior piece. Stitch the remainder of the seam, backstitching at the beginning and end.

Open the zipper all the way and lay out the exterior piece with the right side up.

Step 5. Putting it all together:

Lay the interior out flat, open the zipper pocket half-way, and place the interior piece right side down on the flattened exterior, aligning the outer edges. Finger-press the separating zipper seam flat so that the raw edge of the fabric (stitched to the zipper) extends outward and matches up with the raw edges of the interior. Flip the excess end of the zipper tape outward.

Stitch all the way around, leaving a 3" gap at the zipper head (using a ¼" seam allowance).

Trim the seam allowance and excess zipper tape and turn the clutch right side out, tucking in the seam allowance of the lining at the opening. Slip-stitch the opening closed.

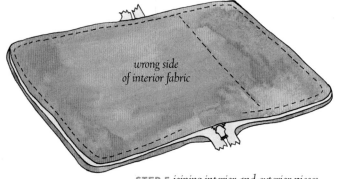

wrong side of interior fabric

STEP 5 *joining interior and exterior pieces*

CLUTCH TEMPLATE *(Enlarge 200%)*

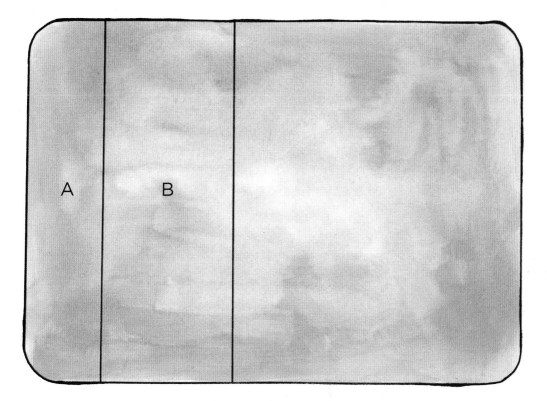

Stitch Smarts

Before you start jabbing yourself with sharp pointy things, let me explain some basic sewing skills that will make your mending adventures safer and, with practice, quicker. I enjoy mending, but the faster I get through the mending pile, the better.

Handiwork

Working by hand is portable and precise. It's perfect for mending on the go, but it takes quite a bit more time than mending on a sewing machine. Personally, I love the process. Slow or fast, hand sewing is what I use for most fixes, but if it's a project I want to get through quickly, I hop over to my studio and stitch it up quickly on "the beast."

Threading a Needle

Before you begin doing any kind of fancy stitching, you start by sticking the thread through the eye of the needle. No matter the size of your work, it's important that the length of your thread is no longer than the length of your arm (about 20"). If you are doubling the thread for stitching things like buttons, snaps, and hooks, it should be almost twice the length of your arm (about 40"). Why? If your thread is too long, it will get tangled, break, knot, and be a general pain. As you stitch, the fabric causes friction on the thread, so after a foot or so of stitching, the thread will start to fray, unravel, and snag. Sewing should be fun, so keep that thread the length of your arm or shorter. Here are two ways to thread a needle.

Eyeballing it: Cut a piece of thread the desired length. Make a clean cut, at an angle, so it's easier to pass the thread through the needle eye. Hold the thread between your forefinger and thumb and guide it through the eye of the needle. Pull it through from the other side.

With a needle threader: A needle threader can be handy, especially when you are first learning to sew. It makes it a snap to stick thread through that tiny little hole. Cut a piece of thread the desired length, making a clean cut at an angle. Feed the point of the needle threader wire through the eye of the needle. Guide the thread through the wire loop of the threader, then pull the wire threader back through the eye of the needle. Remove the threader.

EYEBALLING IT   USING A NEEDLE THREADER

Knotting or Not

Before you start sewing, decide whether or not to knot your ends. If you choose not to make a knot, you can work several small stitches on top of each other to secure the thread's end. If you decide to make a knot, here are some guidelines.

Tying a knot: Take the end(s) of the thread and make a small loop around the tip of your index finger. Pinch the loop with your thumb. Slide the end of the thread through the loop. Tighten the knot by sliding it toward the end of the thread, ideally about ¼" from the end. If the knot isn't big enough, make another one and slide it over the first, then tighten it. Trim the end(s) of the threads as needed. Don't worry if it takes a few attempts to make a knot correctly. Once you get it right, it only takes a second to knot your thread and get started sewing.

SINGLE OR DOUBLE?

When do you use double thread vs. single thread?
DOUBLE THREAD is for sewing on buttons, snaps, and hooks/eyes.
SINGLE THREAD is for sewing seams and hems.

TYING A KNOT

IF SEWING WITH A DOUBLE THREAD *Pull the thread through the needle so both ends are even with each other. Knot the ends together.*

IF SEWING WITH A SINGLE THREAD *Pull the thread through the needle so one end is about half the length of the longer end. Knot the longer end.*

Removing Stitches

Before you even start mending, you often have to take out quite a few damaged stitches. Think of it as a fresh start. While a seam ripper is the easiest to use, you can also use embroidery scissors. I'm always using my seam ripper. I've also become pretty handy with the little scissors attached to my needle book. No wonder my grandma had eight seam rippers around her sewing room. Here are your options for removing stitches.

With a seam ripper: Slip the pointed tip of the seam ripper under a stitch in the seam, between the two fabrics that are sewn together. Push the sharp curved edge of the blade against the thread to cut it. Repeat every fourth stitch or so. To speed up the process, use the tip of the seam ripper to pick loose stitches from the top of the fabric.

With embroidery scissors: Open the scissors and use one point to cut the thread and remove stitches in the same manner as the seam ripper. Only use the tip of the scissors to avoid accidently cutting the fabric.

With a straight pin: For very small or very tight stitches, which can happen by accident if the tension on your machine is off, use a straight pin to loosen stitches before cutting them with a seam ripper or scissors.

Handling the Needle and Thread

If you've not done much sewing, holding and manipulating the needle and thread might feel awkward at first. The more you sew, the more comfortable you'll feel. Everyone has their own way of doing things, but here are some general guidelines:

•→ Hold the needle in your dominant hand, between your thumb and index finger. Use your index finger (this is where you'll want a thimble) to push and guide the needle. Oh yes, thimbles. They are not just a thing of the past. At first, I wasn't too keen on them. But trust me, after a couple of hours of hand sewing, you will wish you had one protecting the tip of your finger. Those little sewing needles have quite the bite after you've worked a hundred or so stitches.

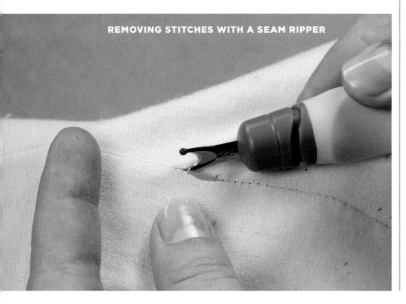

REMOVING STITCHES WITH A SEAM RIPPER

•◆ Hold the fabric in your other hand, with your thumb on top and your fingers bracing it from the bottom.

•◆ Sew from right to left if you are right-handed, and from left to right if you are left-handed.

•◆ To avoid tangles, draw the thread all the way through every time you work a stitch (except for running stitches).

Securing Threads

There is nothing more frustrating to me than taking the time to sew a patch, fix a zipper, or sew on a button only to have it come apart again as soon as there is any stress on the area. So how do you make your stitches stay put? Usually, I make a double loop knot at the end of my work to secure it, but I'll show you three methods for securing thread. Regardless of the method, fasten off your thread when you still have about 3" to 4" left.

Double loop knot: Make a small stitch into your work in an inconspicuous spot, but before pulling the thread all the way through, insert your needle into the loop and also in the resulting second loop.

Cinch up the thread to make a small knot. Clip the thread to release your needle from the work.

Backstitching: Work four or five small backstitches over the top of the last stitches. Stitch through the back of the backstitches, tightly, two or three times. Trim the threads.

Double overhand knot: Leave the thread at least 3" long, then tie it, and tie it again. Trim the ends.

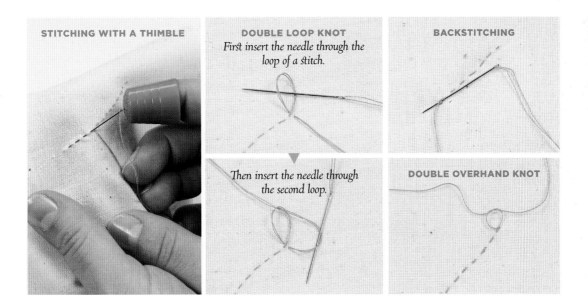

STITCHING WITH A THIMBLE

DOUBLE LOOP KNOT
First insert the needle through the loop of a stitch.

Then insert the needle through the second loop.

BACKSTITCHING

DOUBLE OVERHAND KNOT

Hand Stitches for Every Occasion

*T*here are more types of *stitches* than you can imagine, especially when you discover embroidery stitches. For some decorative embroidery stitches, see page 187. But for mending, you will mostly use the following stitches.

Whip Stitch
(a.k.a. Overcast Stitch)

The whip stitch is a really versatile stitch. You can use it to join seams or to quickly fasten off loose thread in a hole, as in the quick hole fix on page 67. You can also use it to quickly bind two pieces of fabric together.

Step 1. Secure the thread to the back side of your work about ⅛" from the edge, bringing the needle to the front. If working with two layers, as when sewing a seam, secure the thread between the two layers so it will be hidden.

Step 2. Bring the needle around to the back side of the work and push through to the front, ⅛" from the edge. Repeat several times until the length of the edge has been worked.

Slip Stitch
(a.k.a. Blind Stitch)

The blind stitch is the contemporary favorite for fixing up hems by hand quick and easy. The purpose of the slip stitch — also called a blind stitch, hem stitch, or blind hem stitch — is to hold the folded and pressed edge of the hem in place. It's fairly invisible from the right side of the fabric.

Step 1. Secure the knot underneath the folded hem and bring the needle to the front. Catch just a small amount of the bottom fabric with the needle.

Step 2. Make another stitch ½" from the last stitch by catching a small amount of the folded fabric and then the

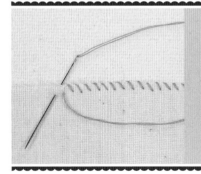

WHIP STITCH TIPS

➵ You can use your finger to nudge the stitches into place so they all line up.

➵ Try to make all your stitches the same length and distance apart.

➵ If you are going to be able to see the stitches and want them to absolutely line up, use a fading fabric marker to mark out a stitch line.

bottom fabric. Repeat for the length of the hem.

Step 3. Use the double loop knot to fasten off the thread.

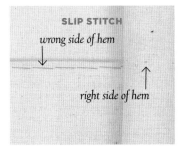

SLIP STITCH
wrong side of hem

right side of hem

Running Stitch

The running stitch is the first stitch I ever learned how to make. I think it was my mom who taught me the amazing wonder of dipping my needle into the fabric several times before pulling it through. It's a versatile stitch that can be worked small for a seam or long for an easy basting stitch.

RUNNING STITCH TIP

If you want a neat line of straight stitches, it's best to take a ruler and your favorite temporary marking tool and draw a nice crisp line to guide you.

Step 1. Secure the thread to the back of the fabric. Make a small stitch. The length of the stitch doesn't really matter; about $1/8$" is good. It depends on the project.

Step 2. With the needle at the back of the work, bring the tip of the needle up through the fabric one stitch length away from the first stitch. Pass the thread over the fabric for a stitch length before taking up another stitch. Repeat this step several times before pulling the thread all the way through so you complete several stitches at one time. Keep the stitches and the spaces between them small and even.

Step 3. As you draw the needle through, pull the thread slightly so the stitches have a nice even tension.

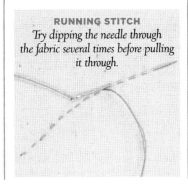

RUNNING STITCH
Try dipping the needle through the fabric several times before pulling it through.

A PASSION FOR MENDING

There is a booklet called "When Mother Lets Us Sew" from the 1920s. It's a wonderful little book filled with useful sewing skills and children's doll patterns. Right after the section on the running stitch there is a little nursery rhyme that reads:

When I'm a grown-up woman,
With my hair up on my head,
I'll sit and sew 'til very late
And never go to bed.

As old-fashioned as that sounds, here I am, stitching away at one o'clock in the morning with my hair pulled back onto my head. Odd how these little poems ring so true, even after 100 years. Not much has changed in mending since then.

The proper sitting position

Basting Stitch

The basting stitch is worked exactly the same as a running stitch, only longer. It's used to hold things in place until you're ready to make the final, more secure stitches.

Backstitch
(a.k.a. Outline Stitch)

For strength, most seams are stitched on a sewing machine, but if one isn't available, this stitch is just as strong. A running stitch should only be used on light seams that don't endure a lot of stress, but a backstitch can be used to seam just about anything. A simple way to remember a backstitch is "one stitch back, two forward."

Step 1. Secure the thread with a knot on the back of the fabric; then bring the needle to the front by drawing it through the fabric. To make it easier, you might want to mark the stitching line with a temporary marking pen.

Step 2. Take a stitch length, about 1/8" long, backward on the marked line. Insert the

needle, and then work a single stitch that is two lengths forward. Draw the needle through to the front of the work.

Step 3. Repeat step 2 to complete a series of backstitches.

Prick Stitch

Similar to a backstitch, the prick stitch is made by working one stitch back and three stitch lengths forward. A tiny stitch is the only thing visible from the front of the work, making it excellent for sewing zippers by hand and giving collars a finished look.

Step 1. Secure the thread with a knot on the back; then bring the needle to the front by drawing it through the fabric.

Step 2. Take a stitch length backward, 1/16" long, on the marked or imaginary stitching line, insert the needle, and then work a stitch three lengths forward. Draw the needle through to the front of the work.

Step 3. Repeat step 2 to complete a series of prick stitches.

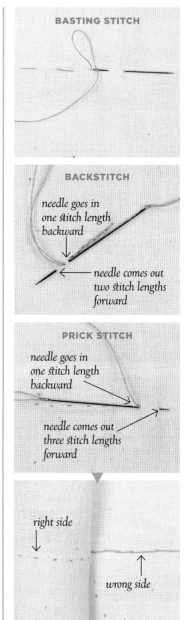

BASTING STITCH

BACKSTITCH

needle goes in one stitch length backward

needle comes out two stitch lengths forward

PRICK STITCH

needle goes in one stitch length backward

needle comes out three stitch lengths forward

right side

wrong side

Cathie Jo, of bo betsy, applied her own loose interpretation of eyelet embroidery and buttonhole stitch to turn the holes in her jean jacket into a fun embellishment that also prevents them from growing larger. She used embroidery floss and needle to hand-stitch these effects.

Ladder Stitch

This stitch works great for closing up any seams that are left open after turning your project right side out.

Step 1. Secure the thread with a knot on the inside of one of the folded edges.

Step 2. Make a small stitch into the opposite folded edge. Cross back to the first folded edge and take another small stitch. Keep repeating to make a ladder of stitches between the two folded edges.

Step 3. Pull on the thread to tighten up the stitches. This will close the gap and make the stitch work invisible.

Buttonhole Stitch and Blanket Stitch

These two stitches are worked the same way; the only difference is the spacing. Buttonhole stitches are worked closer together than blanket stitches.

Step 1. Secure the thread on the back of the fabric.

Step 2. Bring the needle to the front around the raw edge.

Step 3. Insert the needle into the fabric and catch the loop of thread, as shown. Gently pull to tighten the stitch around the edge.

Step 4. Repeat steps 2 and 3 until all of the raw edge has been covered. Fasten off the thread.

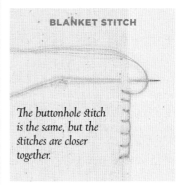

BLANKET STITCH

The buttonhole stitch is the same, but the stitches are closer together.

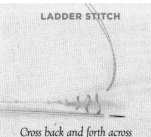

LADDER STITCH

Cross back and forth across folded edges of fabric, picking up small stitches.

THE INDUSTRIAL REVOLUTION — A GREAT LABOR-SAVER

It was a good peach-basket full of mending work. "The mountain has gained upon me a little in these past, busy weeks," said Jane cheerily, "but you will see it speedily reduced to a mole-hill. In the first place, I will oil the sewing machine thoroughly and wind about half a dozen bobbins. Let me see," and she surveyed her pile critically. "Two white bobbins, one of black, and one of brown, and one of gray. That will answer for all the work. You can see how much the machine will help on the work. I call it a great labor-saver, even for the mending-basket."

— Olive (Reader story submitted to *Arthur's Home Magazine*, Volume 52, 1884)

Sewing Machine Stitches

The sewing machine is capable of some fabulous stitches, but straight and zigzag machine stitches are the mainstay of mending.

Straight Stitch

This stitch is great for seams, topstitching, attaching lace, attaching pockets, and a million other things. Shorten the stitch length for lightweight, fine fabrics and loosen it slightly for heavier and bulky fabrics. If you lengthen the stitch a lot, it's a basting stitch.

Zigzag Stitch

This stitch helps finish edges, reinforce fabric, apply elastic, and sew stretch fabrics. It can even be used to darn fabric.

Overlock Stitch

Some sewing machines are capable of an overlock stitch, which overcasts the cut edge, much like the hand overcast stitch. Or, if you are lucky enough to own a serger, you can overlock and trim the fabric edge at the same time.

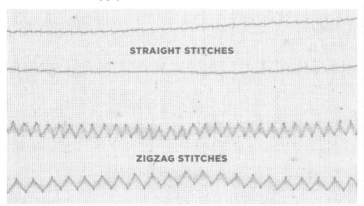

STRAIGHT STITCHES

ZIGZAG STITCHES

STITCH SMARTS NEEDLE BOOK

by Kristin Roach

I like to have a special book of needles just for my mending. It sits open nicely while I work so I can easily switch out safety pins and straight pins, grab a different needle, or tuck the whole thing away so I don't have loose sharps on the table. For me, this needle book is all about safety. Okay, safety and cuteness. Making a needle book is a delight because all you need are a few bits of this and that, and you can make this project in under a half hour. Personalize it for yourself or your friends; it's a great gift for any sewing buddy.

What You'll Need

Scraps of fabric, felt, and stiff interfacing

1 sew-on snap, ¼"

Leaf template

Mending supply kit (see page 24)

Embroidery needle and floss

LEAF TEMPLATE

What You'll Do

Step 1. Cut out the following pieces:

A. Outside of book, from plain woven fabric: one 2¼" × 4¾" piece

B. Inside of book, from plain woven fabric: one 2¾" × 4¾" piece

C. Interfacing: two 2¼" × 2" pieces

D. Felt "pages": one 2¼" × 4¼" piece

E. Leaf template: cut two pieces from fabric (one to match inside of book and one of decorative fabric to match

embellishments) and one from interfacing

F. Optional: scraps of fabric and strip of lace or other trim for embellishment

Step 2. Embellish the fabric for the outside of the book as desired. I decided to make a little globe tree with embroidered leaves and added a strip of lace, but choose any design you like. Leave ¼" undecorated around all the edges, because they will be covered with blanket stitches when we put this little guy all together.

Step 3. To make the needle pleats, mark two parallel fold lines with a fabric marker on piece B. Mark the first line

approximately ¾" from the bottom and the second line ¾" from the first line. Fold and press the fabric along first line. Stitch a line of straight stitches or backstitches ⅛" from the fold. Repeat for remaining marked fold line. Press the top pleat upward and the bottom pleat downward.

Step 4. To make the leaf closure tab, trim the "stem" off of the interfacing piece; then layer the pieces together with the interfacing in the middle and the right sides of the fabric facing away from the interfacing. Work a blanket stitch (see page 52) around the leaf shape, through all the layers. Outline the leaf shape just inside of the blanket stitches with a small running stitch.

Step 5. Pin the pieces together in the following order, then work a blanket stitch around the edges of all the pieces:

❧ Outside cover (A), right side down.

❧ Interfacing pieces (C) lined up at the short edges, leaving a narrow gap in the center.

❧ Leaf tab, off to the right side with the decorative side facing down and just the tab between pieces A and C.

❧ Inside piece (B), right side up.

Step 6. Center the felt piece (D) on the inside of the book, and sew a line of backstitching vertically through all of the pieces.

Step 7. Sew the ball half of the snap to the inside of the leaf. Fold the leaf to line it up with the front of the book. Mark the position for the socket side of the snap and stitch it in place. Fill the book with needles and pins, and you are all set. I like to put different types of sewing needles in the pleats and straight pins in the felt pages.

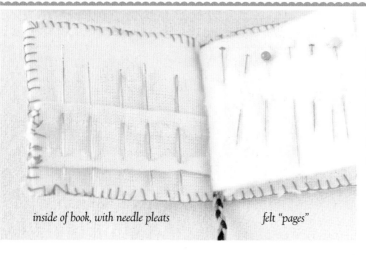

inside of book, with needle pleats   *felt "pages"*

INSPIRATION

I once saw a vintage needle book that had little fabric pleats for the needles to slide through. When you buy needles in packs, they come that way, but the inside of the packs are made from card stock, not fabric.

Adding a Braid

This step is functionally optional, but it sure does look nice, so I would include it if I were you. To make the braid:

➼ Cut three lengths of embroidery thread, each 8" long.

➼ Knot all three lengths of the thread together ½" from the end of the threads.

➼ Use a safety pin to hold the knotted end to a pillow or even your jeans.

➼ Braid the threads together.

➼ Knot the end and trim the ends to ½". Fan out the ends.

➼ Fold the braided embroidery floss in half over the top center of the needle book so it lies in the fold. Work a few stitches at the top of the needle book to keep the embroidery floss in place. Tie the ends at the bottom of the book, or make a few stitches to tack the ends of the braid in place.

You can embellish your needle book with trim, like this lace seam binding.

The braid is a nice decorative accent.

Patchwork

Ah, patchwork. It's functional and fun. Usually when I patch my clothing, I like to let the patches shine by using brightly patterned fabrics and embroidered stitching. On a functional level, there are two main reasons you would apply a patch to your clothes: to extend the life of the fabric by reinforcing it and to replace fabric that is torn, frayed, or missing. This chapter will give you all kinds of ideas for functional and creative patching.

Do It Your Way

For structural and laundering reasons, it's a good idea to use a patch made of fabric that is similar to the type of fabric you are mending: denim for denim, and silk for silk. But that's a suggestion more than a rule. I have used quilt fabric for mending my silk, and silk for mending my jeans. Sometimes the contrasting texture can be just as dynamic as a contrasting color. On the other end of the spectrum, you can place your patch on the inside of a garment to make it less noticeable if you want to preserve the original look of the garment.

Like New

For patches that won't call attention to themselves, use fabrics that match the fabric you are mending and stitch them to the inside of the garment (if extra garment fabric is available). Some pointers:

➸ Fold under the raw edges of the hole and match up the fabric pattern on the patch with the fabric pattern on the garment.

➸ If you can't match the thread color exactly, choose thread that is one shade darker

than the garment's main color; it will show up less than a lighter shade.

➸ Use precise hand-sewing techniques like the blind stitch (see page 48) instead of working on a sewing machine.

Creative Patchwork

To make a statement, choose a patch from a contrasting colored fabric so it will really stand out. As my first-year drawing teacher always said, "Do it or don't do it, but make sure everyone knows it was a choice and not just happenstance." Things to ponder:

➸ If you are going to use a patch as a decorative element, consider the size and shape of the patch. Think about using a fun shape, like the project on page 68, instead of just a rectangle or circle.

➸ Also think about working in multiples, like the patchwork pictured on page 58. If the placement of the tear is in an odd spot, using multiple patches in the same area or on other parts of the garment can look more like a design element than hiding a hole or stain.

TIPS AND TRICKS

❧ If you don't press under the edges of your patch, you can prevent them from fraying by applying fray prevention glue, zigzag stitching the edges, or working a blanket stitch around the edges.

❧ No matter what patch method you use, always wash your patched clothing on the gentle cycle to prevent further damage to your overly loved clothing.

❧ Sometimes areas needing repair are difficult to reach by machine. Consider using hand-sewing techniques for damaged areas in the legs of pants or sleeves of shirts.

❧ Though it's a little extra work at the start, if you reinforce an area as soon as you notice it is wearing thin, you will save yourself a lot of time in the long run.

The advantage of a fusible patch is that it can be applied easily for quick repairs and then stitched down later when you get the chance. If you are only reinforcing a worn area, you don't even have to stitch it into place. Rounding the corners of the patch before applying it will help keep it from peeling off. The downside of a fusible patch is that it doesn't last as long as a stitched-on patch, especially if it's applied to an area that has a lot of stress.

It's often hard to find fusible patches in the store that match your mending project perfectly, or even close to perfectly. Good thing for you and me that it's really easy to make them. I like keeping a little double-sided, paper-backed fusible webbing in my mending bag for just this purpose. Simply press the tacky side of the webbing to the wrong side of the patch of fabric, peel away the paper, and apply it as you would any other fusible patch.

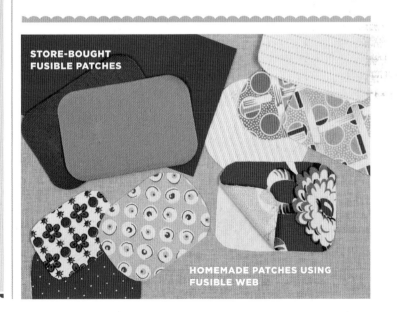

STORE-BOUGHT FUSIBLE PATCHES

HOMEMADE PATCHES USING FUSIBLE WEB

Patching on the Outside

Step 1. Set the iron to the heat temperature required by the garment's care instructions and press the area where you will be applying the patch so it's nice and flat.

Step 2. Trim any stray threads around the hole so the fusible patch has clean contact with the fabric.

Step 3. Cut the fusible patch so it's ½" larger on all sides than the damaged area.

Step 4. Position the patch in place and press it firmly for a few seconds, using a pressing cloth to protect your iron from any stray fusible material. Check to make sure the fusible

Line up patterns of patch and cloth.

FUSIBLE PATCH ON THE OUTSIDE

web's glue has melted enough by trying to lift one corner. If the corner comes up, press again for a few more seconds. Wait until the patch has cooled before wearing the garment.

Patching on the Inside: to Reinforce

If you just have a small damaged area or a place where the fabric is starting to wear thin (knees and elbows are the likely culprits), you can apply a fusible patch to the inside with ease. Just turn the garment wrong side out and follow the same steps for placing a patch on the outside. The patch will provide some extra structure to the damaged area and will extend the life of the garment for quite a few more wears at the very least.

Patching on the Inside: to Match

When patching to match your garment's fabric, you want the patch to be inconspicuous. A good solution is to fuse similarly colored fabric to the inside of a garment. Here's how:

Step 1. Set the iron to the right heat temperature (as required by the garment's care instructions) and press the area where you will be applying the patch so it's nice and flat.

Step 2. Trim any stray threads around the hole so the fusible patch has clean contact with the fabric.

Step 3. Cut the fabric patch ½" larger on all sides than the hole to be patched.

Step 4. Trace the patch shape onto a piece of fusible web and cut it out. Place the web beneath the hole and use a fabric marker to trace the outline of the hole onto the fusible web. Cut out the hole shape and set it aside.

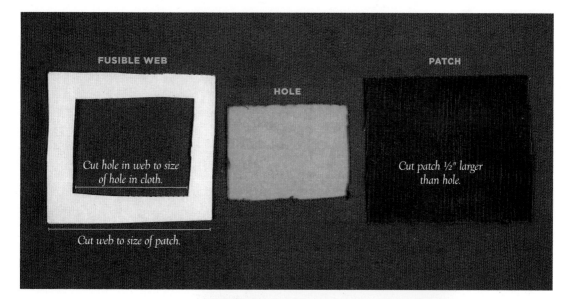

FUSIBLE WEB

HOLE

PATCH

Cut hole in web to size of hole in cloth.

Cut patch ½" larger than hole.

Cut web to size of patch.

Step 5. Position the fusible web ring (with the hole cut out) on the right side of the patch so the outer edges align and then position the patch under the hole, so that there is no fusible web visible in the hole area; press firmly for several seconds.

Step 6. Check to make sure the fusible web's glue has melted enough by trying to lift one corner. If the corner comes up, press for a few more seconds. Wait until the patch has cooled before wearing the garment. If the garment fabric tends to fray, apply fray

APPLYING THE PATCH

prevention glue to the edges of the hole, but test it first on a seam allowance to make sure it doesn't discolor the fabric.

For her embroidered patchwork, Leah Peterson begins by putting a piece of brightly colored or printed fabric behind the hole or tear and hand-basting it in place. Then she cuts the hole into a shape such as a heart, star, or other inspiration of the moment. Finally, she embroiders around the shape with contrasting thread, using running stitches, satin stitches, French knots, and others to make the patch a work of art.

Jamie Smith got her inspiration for what she calls her "crazy patch" style from a seamstress in China. Placing scraps of fabric behind the holes, she simply starts up her machine and stitches over the worn spots like crazy. In just five minutes, her jeans display this scribbled look.

Cloth Patches

By using a cloth patch, you open up many options for decoration as well as concealment. When placing the patch on the outside, use fabric that contrasts the garment. Make it a decoration instead of just trying to hide a hole. The following methods involve stitching instead of fusing, but otherwise the process is similar.

Patching on the Outside

Step 1. Set the iron to the heat temperature required by the garment's care instructions, and press the area where you will be applying the patch so it's nice and flat.

Step 2. Trim any stray threads around the hole to be patched.

Step 3. Cut the patch fabric ½" larger on all sides than the hole to be patched. If you are using lightweight fabric or fabric that frays a lot, add 1"

all around so you can turn the edges to the wrong side for a more finished look.

Step 4. If you are using a machine:

→ Sew a zigzag stitch around the edge of the damaged area to help prevent further fraying.

→ Pin the patch over the hole and zigzag stitch around the edge. If you are using a light-weight fabric, turn the edges of the patch under before applying it for a finished look.

If you are sewing by hand:

→ Work a whip stitch (see page 48) around the damaged area. This serves the same purpose as the zigzag stitch in machine stitching.

→ Pin the patch in place and use a blanket stitch (see page 52) to secure it to the garment and give the patch a finished edge.

Patching on the Inside

Step 1. Set the iron to the heat temperature required by the garment's care instructions, and press the area where you

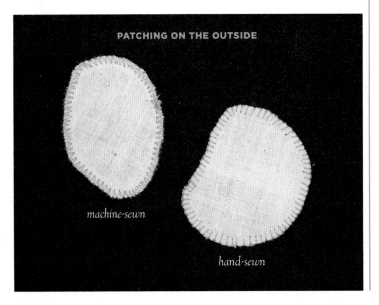

PATCHING ON THE OUTSIDE

machine-sewn

hand-sewn

will be applying the patch so it's nice and flat.

Step 2. Trim any stray threads around the hole to be patched.

Step 3. Neaten the opening into a rectangle shape and cut ¼" notches in the corners so you can turn the raw edges to the inside easier. Fold the raw edges of the hole under and press.

Step 4. Cut the fabric patch ¼" larger on all sides than the hole to be patched so it lines up with the turned-under fabric.

Step 5. With the garment right side out, pin the patch in place with the right side of the patch facing the wrong side of the garment, aligning any pattern in the patch and garment fabrics. Hand-baste to hold the patch in place.

Step 6. Turn the garment wrong side out so you can sew the raw edges of the patch to the turned-under edges of the hole. If you are stitching by machine, use a zigzag stitch to catch the edge of the patch and the turned-under edge. If you are sewing by hand, use a whip

stitch to attach the patch to the turned-under edge. Be careful not to catch the garment outer fabric in the machine stitching. Tack the edges of the patch to the outer fabric with a prick stitch (see page 50).

PATCHING ON THE INSIDE

Fold and press raw edges of hole.

Baste patch to cloth.

Sew patch on and secure with a prick stitch

Quick Fix for a Small Hole

I use this technique for small holes and tears in out-of-the-way spots. It's my favorite hand-mending technique and I use it more than any other.

Step 1. Pick out a fabric that is similar in type and pattern to the garment you are mending and cut it so it's about ½" larger all around than the tear or hole.

Step 2. Use a whip stitch (see page 48) to stitch around the raw edge of the hole.

Step 3. Use a backstitch (see page 50) to stitch the patch to the garment.

QUICK FIX

SWEET PEA FLOWER PATCH

by Pam Harris

This little embellished appliqué is a perfect fix for repairing tears or covering stains. The damaged area is easily covered with a fusible patch or hemmed appliqué. Then, add a simple folded fabric flower to give the patch three-dimensional interest. And finally, fill the center with selvage strips bound into a pompom or covered with a pretty button.

What You'll Need

Flower and circle templates

2 pieces of scrap fabrics in contrasting colors and patterns

Fusible web scraps (optional)

Selvage edges cut from scrap fabrics, for the pompom, or large button (1" diameter)

Mending supply kit (see page 24)

Sewing machine (optional)

What You'll Do

Step 1. For the flat background flower, cut a simple appliqué using the flower pattern provided. If you plan to attach the appliqué with fusible web, cut the patch the exact size as the template (or any size you want) and follow the instructions on page 62 to attach the flower to the garment. If you prefer to sew it in place, cut the flower patch ¼" larger to allow for a hemmed edge and follow the instructions on page 66 to attach it.

Step 2. Make a folded fabric flower:

➻ Use the circle template to trace five circles onto the fabric (for the petals) and cut them out.

FLOWER AND CIRCLE TEMPLATES

◗✦ Thread a needle with 18" of sewing thread, and knot it into a double strand (see page 47).

◗✦ Fold the first circle in half and make a running stitch along the curved raw edges opposite the fold. Be sure to catch both pieces of the fabric in the stitches.

◗✦ To gather the fabric, hold the thread in one hand and slide the fabric toward the knot with the other hand.

◗✦ Continue folding circles and gathering them onto the same length of thread until all five petals have been added.

◗✦ Push the needle into the edge of the first petal and pull the gathered petals into as tight a circle as possible. Secure the thread by taking several tiny stitches in the edge of the first petal. Cut the thread.

Step 3. Sew the folded flower to the center of the flower appliqué with a double-knotted length of thread and tiny stitches through the folded flower, flower appliqué, and garment. Use thread that matches the fabric so the stitches don't show.

Step 4. To hide the center hole of the flower, you can sew a button right over it. Or, make a pompom center from selvage scraps:

◗✦ Cut 40 selvage edges from scrap fabrics, ³⁄₁₆" wide × 2" long.

◗✦ Divide the selvage pieces into four stacks of ten each.

◗✦ Using doubled thread, hold one of the stacks tightly and take about five small stitches through the center of the stack to secure. Do not cut the thread.

◗✦ With the same thread, attach the remaining stacks on top of the first, one at a time, rotating them around the center point (see illustration).

◗✦ Trim the ends of the strips so that they are even. The finished length will be about 1¾".

◗✦ Attach the stack to the garment by inserting the needle through the center of the folded flower and into the garment at the center of the flat flower patch. Pull the pompom tightly against the garment and stitch it in place with a few stitches.

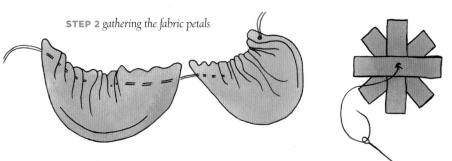

STEP 2 *gathering the fabric petals*

STEP 4 *stitching together the four stacks of strips for pompom to evenly fill out the flower*

MOLA APPLIQUÉ PATCH

by Carina Envoldsen-Harris

This pattern/project is inspired by the mola appliqué technique of the Kuna Indians who live in the San Blas Islands off the coast of Panama. Traditional mola designs are birds, flowers, animals, and devils. It is a reverse appliqué technique with several layers, which are cut through to reveal one or more of the fabrics beneath. Molas are usually very colorful, with solid color fabrics, and a lot of shades of red. Quilting cotton or similar fabrics that aren't too heavy are the easiest fabrics to use. You might want to try the design in the template to learn the technique, and then move on to creating your own designs. It is generally easier to use shapes that are not too angular; sharp corners can be a bit difficult. A pillowcase is a good practice fabric because of its light weight.

What You'll Need

Item to mend
(a pillowcase is shown)

Fabric scraps

Mola templates

Fabric marking pen

Mending supply kit (see page 24)

Sewing machine (optional)

What You'll Do

Step 1. Make a copy of the templates and cut out the largest oval shapes from paper. Use them to trace and cut two or three large ovals per design from different fabrics. (Mola 2 uses two fabrics; the others use three.) Stack the correct number of fabric ovals together accordingly and pin the layers inside the pillowcase, beneath the area you want to mend. Baste around the perimeter of the ovals, through all the layers.

Step 2. Let's start with Mola 3, to give you the idea. Cut a paper template for Mola 3 along the outermost dashed line to make a slightly smaller oval template. Center it over the basted ovals for Mola 3, trace around it, and set the template aside. Pinch the pillowcase fabric and cut a small slit in the center of the outlined shape through the pillowcase fabric only. Make a second cut to the traced line and carefully cut the pillowcase fabric on the marked lines for about ½" or so. (Your design will be more accurate and your work will be easier if you only cut small snips at a time.) As you make cuts, stitch the top layer to the fabric below it (without folding the edge), using a blanket stitch, gradually revealing the first oval layer of fabric.

STEP 2 *Stitch top layer to fabric below with blanket stitch.*

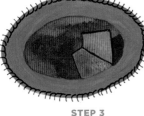

STEP 3

Step 3. Cut the paper template once again along the outermost dashed line. Center and trace this oval onto the exposed layer of fabric. Snip and stitch as in step 2, through the top oval fabric layer only, gradually revealing the second layer of fabric.

Step 4. Cut the paper template on the remaining dashed line and repeat the process, cutting through the second fabric oval to reveal the last fabric layer beneath. Remove the basting layer when finished.

Step 5. For the remaining molas, the placements of the inside shapes are different, but the process is the same. For Mola 1, the top circle is made the same way as Mola 3. For the lower shape, cut through two layers and stitch both as if you were stitching just one.

Step 6. For Mola 2, cut the two oval shapes, place them side by side, and cut and stitch through one fabric layer.

MOLA TEMPLATES

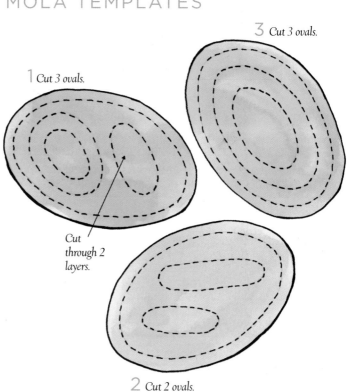

1 *Cut 3 ovals.*

3 *Cut 3 ovals.*

Cut through 2 layers.

2 *Cut 2 ovals.*

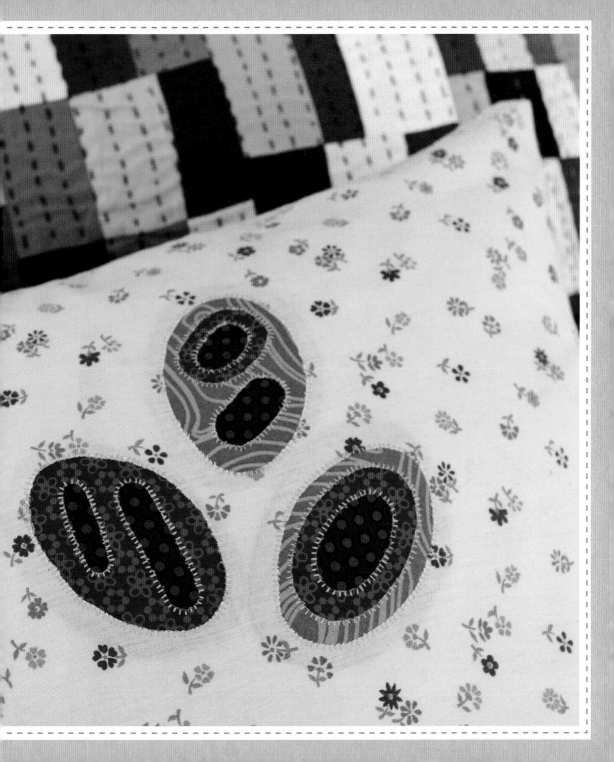

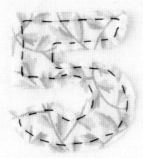

Surface Fixes

When the damage is only on the surface, it's a quick and easy fix. A little snag or a little pull can be quickly righted. A patch pocket can be easily stitched back into place, or even completely replaced without much fuss. Even pleats can be restitched to give them new life. This chapter is a great place to get your mending toes wet. Just the thing you need to confidently dive into seam fixes and eventually have a go at replacing an obnoxious broken zipper.

Snags and Pulls

*W*hile the fabric might not tear completely, when you snag your favorite stockings or sweater, bigger mending problems are soon to arrive. Over time, if you continue to wear them, the snag will become an unsightly run or even a large hole. Happily, snags make for an easy fix and you can prevent further damage. There are three good ways to fix a snag.

Gentle Tugging

If it's a stretch fabric, give it a little tug until the loop goes back into the fabric.

Crochet Hook

For sweaters and other garments made from large, bulky yarns, use a crochet hook to grab the snag. Insert the crochet hook from the back of the item, near the snag, and pull the snag (loose loop of yarn) through the fabric to the wrong side. Do a couple of backstitches (see page 50) over the loop to secure it in place.

Needle or Straight Pin

For fine-threaded fabrics like stockings, T-shirts, and jeans, use a needle to poke the snagged loop of thread to the wrong side. Then, tack it down with several backstitches to secure it in place.

TUGGING GENTLY

USING A CROCHET HOOK

Patch Pocket Fixes

~

*P*atch pockets have a tendency to pull away from a garment near the top of the pocket. Sometimes the stitching that holds the pocket to the fabric starts to fray and come apart from stress. This is particularly true if you, like me, put your fists in your pockets with downward pressure or fill them with pins, paper, knitting needles, and the like. There are a few ways to fix things right up.

Top Edge of a Pocket

Step 1. Trim any loose threads.

Step 2. Use the straight stitch on your sewing machine or the backstitch if you are repairing by hand. Work stitches over the top of one another to tack the corners of the pocket back in place.

Step 3. Continue stitching past the point where the threads unraveled and backstitch to secure both your working thread and the cut thread ends to prevent further unraveling.

Topstitching

Step 1. Trim any loose threads.

Step 2. Stitch over the loose threads or missing stitches by hand with a backstitch or with the straight stitch on your sewing machine.

Step 3. Continue stitching beyond the damaged area so that you topstitch over several stitches that weren't torn or frayed. This will secure the new stitches and prevent any of the old stitches from coming undone. Fasten off your thread.

Patching

It sounds funny, I know — patching a patch pocket — but sometimes your pocket gets a hole and you need to patch it up. Check out chapter 4 for the best ways to patch a hole or tear. If you are fixing a patch pocket on a sweater, chapter 10 will show you everything you need to know to darn your pocket back into a state of excellence.

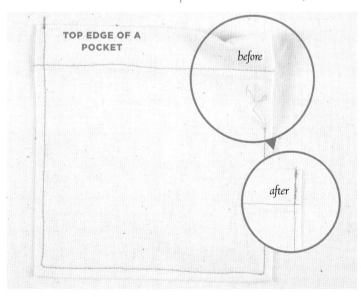

TOP EDGE OF A POCKET

before

after

POCKET CONFESSIONS OF A THRIFT SHOP JUNKIE

by Crispina ffrench

I do most of my clothes shopping at thrift stores for my family and myself. The other day I found the most outrageous zip-up hoodie sweatshirt made of thick red cotton and completely covered with gold sequins. It was a girl's size 7/8. I bought it, thinking I would craft it into something bigger that would fit me, but as soon as my young daughters discovered my bag of loot, they absconded with my treasure and claimed it as their own. Their only disappointment was the fact that there were no pockets, which I was easily able to remedy!

What You'll Need

Thrift store sweatshirt

Remnant of fabric for your pocket made of similar weight and stretch as the sweatshirt

Embroidery floss

Mending supply kit (see page 24)

What You'll Do

Step 1. Using the pocket on a different sweatshirt as a pattern, cut two "kangaroo" shaped pockets. If the edges of your pocket fabric will fray, add ⅝" seam allowance all around. If your pockets are made from a fabric that won't unravel, add ⅝" seam allowance to the curved edges only.

Step 2. Press under the seam allowances.

Step 3. Using embroidery floss, hand-stitch the curved edges with a running stitch to secure the seam allowances to the pockets. The fold at the pocket openings is important so those edges don't stretch.

Step 4. Pin the pockets onto the sweatshirt and sew them down using the same simple running stitch.

THINK OUTSIDE THE BOX

Pockets can be added to lots of garments. I have added cell phone pockets to the inside center back of my running shorts and pants. This placement keeps my shorts from pulling on one side due to the off-center weight of my phone/pedometer/timer. I used T-shirt fabric for these pockets, keeping them soft and absorbent against my skin. These pockets work best if they are just as wide as and a bit deeper than the gadget they are designed to hold to keep them secure even when bouncing around at a full-tilt sprint.

When you decide to add pockets to a pocket-free garment, an important consideration is fabric choice. It's usually best to match the fabric weight and stretch of the garment that is getting pockets.

BUTTON PATCH POCKET

by Susan Beal

I found this skirt at a yard sale and really liked it, but somehow it never found its way into heavy wardrobe rotation. I realized this summer that I'd wear it more often if it just had a pocket! I made a simple-shaped, self-lined patch pocket just big enough to hold my keys, lip balm, and phone. I closed it with a snap and layered two of my favorite vintage buttons in the center as a pretty ornament. For the pocket fabric, I chose a vintage anchor-and-wheel print in the same black and white color scheme as the original skirt fabric, so the pocket pops more than clashes, but I think it would be just as lovely in a solid color or more vivid print.

What You'll Need

Skirt or other garment to update

Remnant of sturdy woven fabric for your pocket (I used a vintage cotton print)

Pocket pattern

1 snap set

2 flat buttons of your choice, in varying sizes and with 2 stitch holes

Mending supply kit (see page 24)

What You'll Do

Step 1. Press the scrap fabric and use the pocket pattern to cut out two pieces. Decide where to place your pocket on the original garment (this is a lovely way to hide a stain or other imperfection). Set the garment aside.

Step 2. Pin the two pocket pieces with the right sides together. Machine-stitch around the curved sides and bottom using a ³⁄₈" seam allowance, backstitching at the beginning and end of the seam. Leave the top edge unstitched. Clip the curves and press the pocket. Turn the pocket right side out and press again.

Step 3. Press under the top edge of the pocket ³⁄₈" so the raw edges are neatly tucked inside and the top edge is smooth, even, and straight. Edgestitch it a scant ⅛" from the edge, backstitching at the beginning and end of the seam.

Step 4. Press the pocket once more and pin it into place on your garment. If your garment is lined (which my skirt was), gently move the lining away from the area you're sewing so it's not caught in the seam. Edgestitch the curved sides

and bottom of the pocket to the garment using a scant ⅛" seam allowance, backstitching at the beginning and end. If you like, add a diagonal stitch to the pocket corners (as shown on the template) for reinforcement. I used chalk to draw a reference line for the diagonal stitching.

Step 5. Mark the center of the pocket top and the corresponding spot on the garment, and hand-sew a snap set in those locations.

Step 6. Hand-sew the larger flat button over the snap stitches. Layer the second button over the first and securely hand-sew that one, too.

POCKET PATTERN

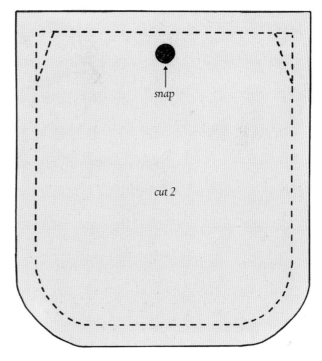

snap

cut 2

VINTAGE SKIRT RE-PLEAT

by Kristin Roach

Quite a while ago I found this really neat pleated skirt made of wool, but the length was a bit long. I opted to shorten the hem so it hit the bottom of my knees, an easy alternation (see page 104). I loved this skirt and wore it every fall and winter. It was perfect with sweaters, tights, cute jackets, woven scarves, and all that other glorious winter attire. Unfortunately, over time, the pleats that I loved started losing their crisp look. It's easy to make pleats crisp looking again, but it takes more than a general pressing. If you want knife-edge pleats like you see on wool kilts, it does take a couple of steps, but nothing that a little patience, a needle and thread, a bit of cardboard, and a seam gauge ruler cannot fix.

Step 1. Refold and press the pleats loosely; do not worry too much about that crisp edge yet. Using a long running stitch, baste the pleat through the fold to the fabric it is folded over.

Step 2. Position the garment on a hard surface. Slip card stock into the pleat and press the pleat on the highest steam setting. Slowly lower the steam setting until the moisture has been removed and you are left with a dry pleat.

Step 3. Repeat pressing for every pleat.

Step 4. Remove the basting stitches.

When Ágnes Palkó's favorite linen
dress developed a couple of small
holes, she mended it with a beautiful,
tightly cross-stitched snail design. She
added a piece of linen embroidery
fabric under the hole first to secure
her stitches.

Seam Fixes

When you rip out a seam in anything, that item is immediately out of commission. For decency's sake, you just cannot wear it any longer without mending it first. Seam fixes are really easy, so don't be sad when the side seam of your favorite shirt rips out. You can restitch, patch, and even alter a garment at the seams without much fuss at all.

Straight Seams

Every mender's dream is a nice straight seam. Fixing a straight seam often takes under five minutes. After you finish stitching and take it off the sewing machine, your clothing is as good as new.

Stitching a Seam

Step 1. Turn the garment wrong side out.

Step 2. Trim any loose threads and rip out any stitches that are not in good repair.

Step 3. Stitch over the unstitched area with a backstitch (see page 50) if you are mending by hand or the straight stitch on your sewing machine.

Step 4. Start stitching before and continue stitching beyond the damaged area, stitching over the good part of the seam for several stitches. Backstitch at the beginning and end of the seam. Fasten off the thread.

Fixing a Seam with Torn Fabric

When the fabric (not the stitching) tears, you need to patch the fabric before you can repair the seam.

Step 1. Rip out the seam stitches along the damaged area (see page 46).

Step 2. Use any method from chapter four to patch the tear. Usually, I reinforce the tear with a little patch of fabric. I pin or fuse the patch to the wrong side of the fabric and zigzag around the edge of the patch and over the tear. You might need to patch the fabric on both sides of the seam; once the stitches are removed you'll have a better idea where the tear is located.

Step 3. Once patched, simply pin the fabric with the right sides together and stitch the seam back together. If you are working with a sewing machine, use the straight stitch; if you are mending by hand use the backstitch (see page 50). They are the best stitches for seam stitching repair.

COLOR POP

When the side seam ripped out, I took the opportunity to add some pops of color to this already bold shirt. Using a little glue stick, I laid out a pleasing arrangement with scraps of fabric and then sewed them in place with a blanket stitch.

FIXING A SEAM WITH TORN FABRIC

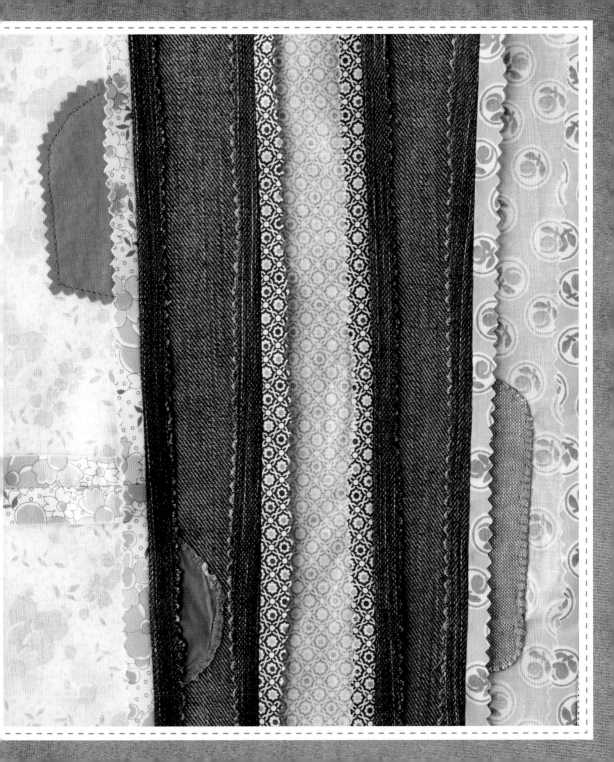

In-Seam Pockets

ockets that are attached to the garment in the seam are easy to fix; eliminate the fear of change falling out of your pocket from inside your coat by simply restitching the pocket seam or stitching over a hole.

Repairing a Hole

If the hole is at the bottom of the pocket, you can resew the seam and make the pocket a little smaller to bypass the hole. If, however, like me, you love big pockets, take the time to patch the hole, using any of the methods from chapter 4 to patch the pocket. I find that working by hand is the easiest way to fix an in-seam pocket without having to take it apart.

REPAIRING A POCKET

Enlarge the seam allowance to bypass the hole.

REPAIR TIP

Keep your hand positioned inside the pocket so you don't accidentally stitch the two sides of your pocket together. Trust me, it's a lot easier to do that than you might think!

Replacing an In-seam Pocket

Sometimes an in-seam pocket is torn beyond patching and needs to be replaced. While it's a little trickier than replacing a patch pocket (see page 80), I know you will be able to do this without any problems.

Step 1. Carefully remove all the stitches surrounding the pocket to remove it from the seam.

Step 2. Use the damaged pocket as a template to cut new fabric, or use the template on page 89. Before cutting, check that the pocket is the right size for your hand. Enlarge the template as needed. Find a fabric of similar weight to the one you are removing. For instance, if you remove a satin pocket, replace it with satin. Cut two pocket pieces from the chosen fabric, adding ½" seam allowances all around.

Step 3. Sew the pocket pieces with the right sides together by stitching all along the curved edges, leaving the straight edge unstitched. Fold the top edge of the pocket and press.

REPLACING A POCKET

Step 2: Use the old pocket as a template.

Step 4. Turn the garment inside out. Fit the new pocket into the seam opening and pin it in place.

Step 5. Use the hand backstitch to stitch the folded edge of the pocket to the opening, adding extra stitches at each corner for a little extra support.

Step 6. Restitch the seam around the pocket, being sure to catch and tack down any loose threads. Turn the garment right side out and you are all set.

Step 4: Pin the pocket in place.

POCKET TEMPLATE

(Enlarge to desired size to fit hand)

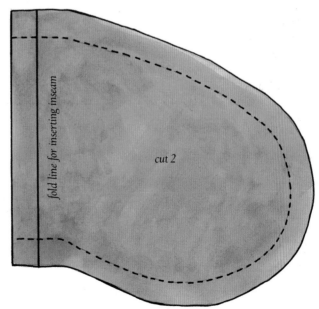

fold line for inserting inseam

cut 2

Altering a Seam

W̶hether it's a bit too loose or a bit too tight, a few simple alterations to the seams of a favorite shirt, pair of paints, or cute
dress can make it feel just right — and make it look great, too!

Taking In a Seam

Step 1. Turn the garment
inside out and slip it on.

Step 2. Pinch the fabric at
the seams and pin it with a few
safety pins.

Step 3. Take the garment off
and tidy up the pinning job so
the seams are even. Pin each
seam approximately the same
amount.

Step 4. Work a basting stitch
along the newly pinned seams.

Step 5. Put the garment back
on and adjust the fit as needed.

Step 6. Take the garment off
again and if you are happy
with the fit, stitch the seams
with more secure stitches,
such as the backstitch if you
are working by hand or a short
straight stitch if you are working by machine.

Step 7. Try it on one more
time and if everything looks
great, go ahead and trim away
the excess fabric at the seams.
Finish the edges with an overlock stitch (see page 53) or
zigzag stitch (see page 53).

*Pin with straight pins while safety
pins are still in place.*

Letting Out a Seam

Before you let out a seam, first
be sure your garment has seam
allowances of at least ½". Here
are the steps:

Step 1. Turn the garment
inside out. Press the seam
allowances together.

Step 2. Use a basting stitch
to sew a new seam in the seam
allowance.

Step 3. Remove the original
seam stitching (see Removing
Stitches on page 46), turn the
garment right side out, and try
it on.

Step 4. If it fits, stitch over
the basting stitches with more
secure stitches, such as the
backstitch if you are working
by hand or a short straight
stitch if you are working by
machine. Press the new seams.

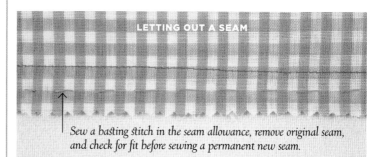

*Sew a basting stitch in the seam allowance, remove original seam,
and check for fit before sewing a permanent new seam.*

SECRET POCKETS

by Kristin Roach

I found the cutest fall jacket at the department store, on sale for just $8. I could not believe my eyes! This cuteness, for only $8? Of course I brought it home with me. Whenever I wore it I always received compliments. Yet, I found I chose to wear a different jacket over and over again. Why was this the case? I wondered this myself. And then it hit me — no pockets! At first I thought patch pockets would be perfect, but because of the jacket style that was out of the question. It wasn't until I started working on this book that I realized I could add pockets after all, in-seam pockets! My jacket was lined, though, so there were a few extra steps to keep the pockets hidden inside.

What You'll Need

Jacket (or other item) that needs a pocket

Lightweight lining fabric for the pocket

In-seam pocket template (see page 89)

Mending supply kit (see page 24)

Sewing machine (optional)

What You'll Do

Step 1. If the hem of your lining is stitched to the jacket, rip out about 4" of stitches along the bottom at the side seams. This gives you some leverage to hold the pocket while sewing it.

Step 2. It is important to position both side seam pockets symmetrically, so measure and mark each side seam the desired distance from the hem to where you want each pocket to go. Mark the top and bottom placement of each pocket, with the distance between the markings at least 4" wide so your hand will fit in.

Step 3. Rip out the stitches between the top and bottom marks on each side seam.

Step 4. Fold the pocket fabric in half and cut two template shapes, creating two pocket pairs (or four single pocket pieces).

Step 5. For each pocket, pin two pieces with the right sides together. Stitch around the curved edge, leaving the straight edge open. Leave the pockets wrong side out.

Step 6. Press the straight, unstitched edge of each pocket to the wrong side to give it a nice finished edge. Clip the seam allowance as needed to make the fold.

Step 7. Pin the pockets into the seam openings you made in step 3, lining up the folded edge of the pocket with the folded edge of the seam.

Step 8. Use the backstitch to secure each pocket in its place, stitching through the seam allowance only so the stitches don't show on the outside.

Step 9. Work a prick stitch (see page 50) to restitch the lining. Work a couple of backstitches at the beginning and the end. That's it. Check out how cute those new pockets are!

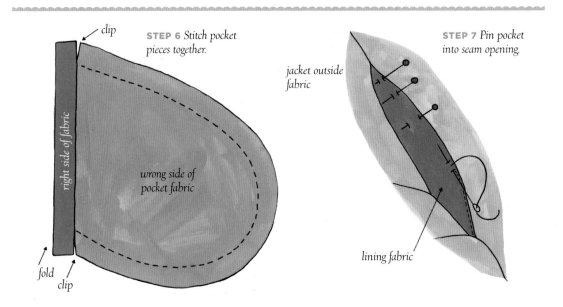

clip

STEP 6 *Stitch pocket pieces together.*

jacket outside fabric

right side of fabric

wrong side of pocket fabric

fold

clip

STEP 7 *Pin pocket into seam opening.*

lining fabric

PROM TO PRINCESS PLAY DRESS

by Stacie Wick

My daughters' godmothers did not come with magic wands. When my little princesses want to go to the ball, the finery must be supplied in a more mundane way. But ready-made dress-up clothes cost more than I am willing to pay, and only smaller sizes are easy to find. Besides, they're not sturdy enough to stand up to a child's enthusiasm. My little girls, like many, are a mixture of sugar and spice. The sugar wants the ruffles, and the spice wants the action. After all, Cinderella didn't casually saunter out of the ballroom when the clock began to strike midnight. She hitched up those skirts and ran for it! And after the last toll of the bell, there was a quick change back into her peasant clothes. But, how do you solve the problems of expense and sturdiness? Enter the outdated prom dress.

Sizing Up the Situation

Remember as you shop and make your selection, that the dress you buy will be refashioned and transformed into dress-up play clothes. Begin by taking a careful look at your choices. Here are some questions that can help you visualize the kind of alterations you may want to make:

- Will you be able to shorten it and use the extra fabric for ruffles?
- Does the skirt have more than one layer, so that the top layer can be scrunched to make a scalloped overskirt?
- Will you need to add or remove straps, sleeves, or boning?
- Are there beads that are going to give you problems when you sew?

What I Did

This project started with a very basic dress. It was sleeveless, knee length, and made of polyester crepe with a full acetate lining. It had princess seaming and a gored skirt, and zipped up the back. Someone had altered this dress before, because the hem was a bit crooked and obviously not the original. That was the first thing I fixed, simply folding it up and hiding it in a new seam. Naturally you'll need to get creative with what you can find, but here's what I did with my prom dress:

- I used my scissors to take it apart at the waist, preserving as much of the serged edge as I could to prevent unraveling.

❧ I left the bodice layers together, simply taking in the seams under the arms. For measurements and proportions, I compared this dress to one that I already knew fit my princess.

❧ I attached decorative ribbon to the bodice with fabric glue.

❧ I separated the overskirt and underskirt. I left the slippery underskirt in one piece, but split the overskirt down the center. I gave it rounded corners and a ruffle, and left it long to make a train. I made the ruffle from the scarf from another dress.

❧ I turned the top edge of the underskirt down to make a casing for elastic before gathering it to fit the bodice.

❧ I sewed both skirts to the bodice about 4" up from the original seam with the right sides together.

❧ Somewhere along the way, I accidentally snipped a small hole in the overskirt, so after mending that with a zigzag stitch and a patch, I hid the mend by tacking the front of the overskirt into swags and adjusting the ruffle.

❧ Elastic through the casing made a nicely gathered waistline (gathers hide many sins).

❧ A gem at the neckline, a crinoline underneath, and there you have it, a dress fit for a fairy-tale princess!

FINDING A GOWN

Don't have a prom or bridesmaid's dress languishing in the back of your closet? Try asking around. If you are fortunate, someone you know will be happy to make a donation. Or, do what I did and go shopping. Check out yard sales and thrift stores. Our neighborhood subdivision holds a yard sale every summer and I found several formal gowns this year. Our local thrift shop keeps out-of-style formal dresses on a special rack in the back, and brings them out to sell as Halloween costumes. I only had to ask, and the attendant was happy to let me peruse the stash out of season. And, don't forget consignment shops.

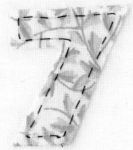

Straight Hems

When you hem your pants, skirt, or even your shirt, it will drastically change the look and feel — I would even say attitude — of your clothing. It could be something as simple as changing the length. When I was a teenager, I used to scour the thrift store for old granny skirts that could be transformed into unique above-the-knee cute skirts. Heck, I suppose I still do.

Repairing Hem Stitches

*H*ems most often tear from dragging on the floor or getting caught in a heel. If you know your pants are too long, save yourself much trouble by taking up your hem before they tear. I have been lazy about that key step when I first get pants and I always regret it. Taking up a hem requires less than 15 minutes of your time. Fixing a torn hem can take around an hour depending on the extent of the damage.

If only your hem's stitching is torn (doesn't need a length adjustment) and it's topstitched, simply use the straight stitch on your sewing machine to fix it. If it's a blind hem (meaning a line of stitches doesn't show on the top of the fabric), use the blind hem setting on your sewing machine or use the lock stitch (see page 99) if sewing by hand. I'll show you what I mean.

Blind Hem by Machine

This stitch, if done correctly, forms a nearly invisible stitched hem. Not every sewing machine is capable of the blind stitch, so check your sewing machine manual. If yours doesn't, don't despair; you can do a blind stitch by hand. The machine blind hem can be a little tricky, so I will walk you through it.

Step 1. Change the presser foot to the blind hem foot and set the sewing machine to the blind stitch setting.

Step 2. Fold the hem to the desired finished length. Place the hem allowance facedown on the table and fold back the

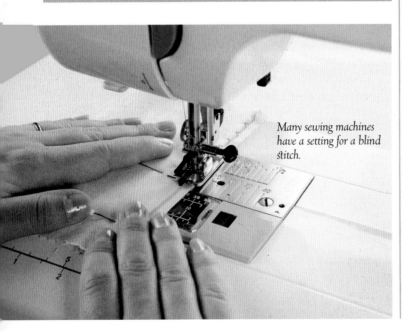

Many sewing machines have a setting for a blind stitch.

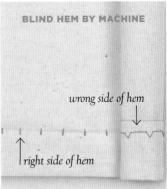

BLIND HEM BY MACHINE

wrong side of hem

right side of hem

rest of the garment, allowing about ¼" of the hem allowance to extend beyond the garment fold; press and pin it in place.

Step 3. Place the fabric under the foot, and line up the fabric fold with the presser foot guide. As you sew, catch the edge of the fold when the needle moves to the left.

Blind Stitch by Hand

The blind stitch is the contemporary favorite for the quick-and-easy way to fix up hems by hand. The purpose of the blind stitch — also called slip stitch, hem stitch, or blind hem stitch — is to hold the folded and pressed edge of the hem in place. It's fairly invisible from the right side of the

fabric. See the Slip Stitch on page 48 for instructions on how to do this stitch.

Lock Stitch by Hand

The lock stitch is perfect for hems, especially if you need the stitching to be as unnoticeable as possible. Because of the way the stitches are worked, if the thread breaks, only the stitches in the immediate area unravel. You can repair just a torn area or a whole hem.

Step 1. Secure the knotted thread on the wrong side with a series of backstitches.

Step 2. Insert the needle through the garment fabric, picking up only a few threads, and then insert it through the hem edge.

Step 3. Draw the needle until it is almost through, and then guide the needle under the connecting thread. Cinch the stitch closed by pulling the thread gently.

Step 4. Repeat steps 2 and 3, working each stitch about ¼" apart and taking care that the stitches don't show on the right side of the garment.

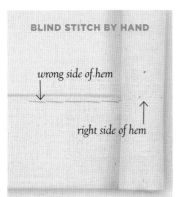

BLIND STITCH BY HAND

wrong side of hem

right side of hem

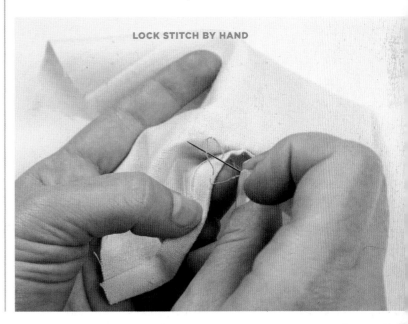

LOCK STITCH BY HAND

When I first saw this skirt it was about 12" longer than it is now. I instantly thought what a fun little flirty skirt it would be short, especially with some leggings, a bulky cabled sweater vest, and some boots. Oh, and in the summer, with a cute little glitzy tank and some strappy sandals. With some dramatic cutting and basic hemming, my skirt had its new look!

Fixing a Torn Hem

If your hem is torn, you have a couple of options. If the tear is from your pants dragging on the floor, you can easily double up the repairs by shortening the hem and restitching it with the damaged area inside the turned-under hem. Or, you can try a patch.

No matter what kind of hem you are repairing, pulling out your iron and ironing board to making a nice crisp hemline makes all the difference in the world. I'm not just talking about looks, though that is very true. It actually makes sewing the hem back to new so much easier.

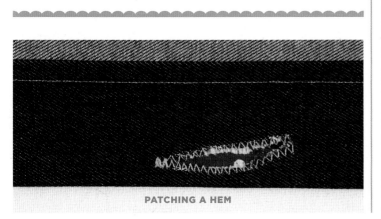

PATCHING A HEM

Patching a Hem

If the damage is large, it's not a problem to patch a hem.

Step 1. Rip out the hem stitches for at least 2" on both sides of the damaged area.

Step 2. Using the method of your choice from chapter 4, patch the damaged area. I like the quick fix option on page 67 because it won't be seen.

Step 3. Fold and press the patched area at the hemline. Restitch the hem through the patched area, using the same method as the original hem. For instance, if the hem was topstitched, topstitch over the patched hem and if it was hand-sewn, then hand-sew the patched area.

If you don't have a lot of extra fabric to work with, you can lengthen a hem by adding a panel of decorative fabric. Using scraps of vintage fabrics, I cut 3" off the bottom of this skirt, and then reattached it to the patchwork panel.

Making a New Hemline

W hether you are letting out a hem or taking it up, you will need to mark where you want your new hem to fall. A second person is very helpful. Why? If you try to mark the hemline while wearing the garment, bending over changes the length. The back of the garment will also become much shorter than the front. Stand straight and tall while your sewing pal marks the new hemline. If you don't have a sewing buddy, safety-pin the hem in several places. Take off the garment and even out the hem allowance by measuring from the old hem.

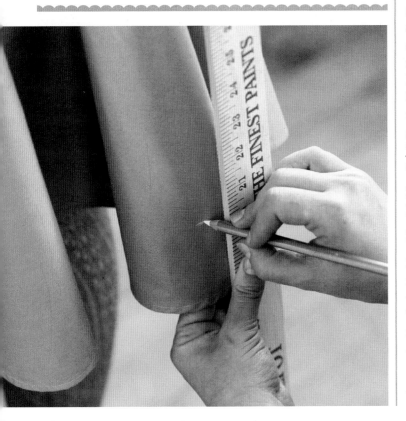

Letting Down a Hem

Usually there is quite a bit of extra fabric folded into a hemline. You can easily add length to a garment by letting out that excess fabric and restitching your hemline.

One time I made myself a super-cute little dress shirt. The idea was that I would wear it over leggings so I wanted it to be a little short. But when I customized the length to fit me a little better, it was somehow much too short. I felt exposed. I felt drafty. Thankfully I had left a generous amount of fabric in the hem so I was able to give myself 2" more coverage, just enough to keep me modest. Here's how you do it.

Step 1. Rip out all the existing hem stitches.

Step 2. Press the crease flat.

Step 3. With the help of a friend, mark where you want the edge of the fabric to fold. Then use a seam gauge to mark an even line around the entire hem.

Step 4. Tuck the raw edge under by ¼". Press. Fold again, aligning it with your marked line. Press.

Step 5. Use the lock stitch if you are hemming by hand or the blind hem setting on your machine to resew the hem.

Taking Up a Hem

Like the granny skirts I used to snatch up from thrift stores, you can make a skirt cute and flirty by taking it up a few inches. I am short, so skirts and pants are always too long on me. If I don't correct the problem up front, my jeans will drag on the ground, get caught under my shoes, and become shredded and worn. Happily, this is a very easy fix to do by hand or on the sewing machine. Among your sewing supplies, be sure to have a seam gauge and an iron. The iron is key because without it you will not be able to make a crisp new hemline.

Taking up a hem is just the same as letting out a hem, except you fold more fabric up instead of letting more fabric down. Follow the instructions on page 103 for Letting Out a Hem, but if you are shortening the garment a lot, you might want to trim away some of the excess hem fabric (evenly), so it's not too bulky.

Follow the instructions on page 103 for Letting Out a Hem

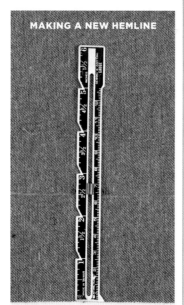

MAKING A NEW HEMLINE

Step 3: marking the fold with the help of a seam gauge

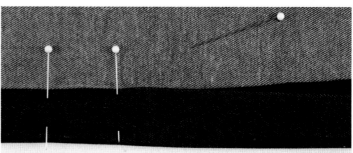

Step 4: tucking the raw edge under, folding again, and pressing flat

QUICK-FIX TIPS

The first time I ever mended any clothing on my own was with duct tape. In fact, I think I wore it like that for months and it still held after several washes. Eventually, I restitched the hem, but that duct tape was perfect in a bind. Duct tape mending showed me that in a pinch, when you don't have time to stitch up that skirt you're planning on wearing to work, tape it up and it should be a-okay for the rest of the day. In some emergency situations, you can even use a stapler to fix a loose stitch or two.

HISTORICAL HEM

by Jennifer Forest

In the nineteenth century, a very young girl wore short skirts just at the knee, and as she aged her skirts would be lengthened. By the time she entered society at the age of 16 or 17, her skirts would be at the fashionable length for an adult. In keeping with the thrifty virtue, many children's shirts, trousers, dresses, and skirts had their hems let down or a new hem added as a child grew. To lengthen a hem, common decorative hem additions included a panel of embroidery, pleated fabric, ribbon strips sewn over a "let down" hem, and decorative trim draped over an extension piece of fabric. All these additions extended the life of a young girl's skirt as she grew. Here is a contemporary take on this practice, which still makes a lot of sense for today's growing girl.

What You'll Need

Skirt or dress

Decorative hem fabric, 9" x the circumference of hem + 8" (or 9" x 2 times the circumference of hem if you want pleats)

Complementary fabric for the trim, 4" x circumference of hem

Mending supply kit (see page 24)

Sewing machine (optional)

What You'll Do

Step 1. Press under a ½" hem on the two long edges of the decorative hem fabric. Stitch in place.

Step 2. Measure and mark the desired locations for four evenly placed inverted pleats. To make each pleat, place a pin at the place that will become the center of the pleat (called the center line). Fold the fabric from about 1" on each side of the pin to meet at the center line (see illustration on following page).

Step 3. Press each pleat and then baste across the top edge of the decorative hem to hold all the pleats in place until they are stitched to the skirt.

Step 4. Trim any excess fabric from circumference and stitch a ½" seam to form a complete circle. Gather top edge if desired.

Step 5. Pin the decorative hem to the skirt, placing it 2" up from the bottom edge. Topstitch the decorative hem onto the skirt edge.

Step 6. To make the trim: Press under a small hem on all four sides of the trim fabric. Fold the long sides of the rectangle into the center and press.

Step 7. Pin the trim, folded side down, above the join of the main hem and skirt. At each pleat, gather the trim in tiny folds. Hand-sew the folds together at each gathering point, then sew the trim to the skirt at each gathering point. (See illustration below)

Step 8. Finish skirt by pressing all seams.

MOVING HEMS IN HISTORY

Before mass-produced clothing, it was common to extend the life of a dress or skirt. A capable woman in the eighteenth or nineteenth century, whatever her station in life, was expected to be able to manage her budget with thrift and economy. They understood the concept of recycling and adapting! Economy was also often a matter of necessity for families living in rural areas, some distance from the linen draper or haberdashery store.

Then, as now, clothes were also adapted with changes in fashion. Women's dresses and skirts often had a bodice line lowered or a hem decorated. In 1807, Jane Austen put "five breadths of linen" into a flounce on her dress to lengthen the hem, because the short skirts that revealed the ankle went out of fashion.

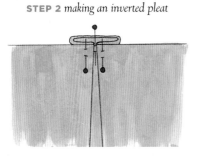

STEP 2 *making an inverted pleat*

STEP 7 *making gathers in trim*

Around the Waist

Some mending takes place around our hips. Loose elastic, snagged belt loops, missing drawstrings — all these things can make a perfectly good pair of our favorite jeans suddenly unwearable. In this chapter, you'll find what you need to fix your waistband quickly. Mending jobs around the waist are some of the easiest to do. Even replacing the elastic on your most comfy pj's can be done in under a half hour.

Elastic Repairs

Elastic bands in clothing come in two fashions, the kind that's stitched directly to the fabric and the kind in a casing where only the ends (if that) are secured to the fabric. Sometimes the elastic comes undone. In that case, simply stretch it back to where it should be, pin it in place, and stitch. Sometimes elastic loses its lovely stretch and the whole piece needs to be replaced. It's still a pretty easy project, but takes a little more know-how.

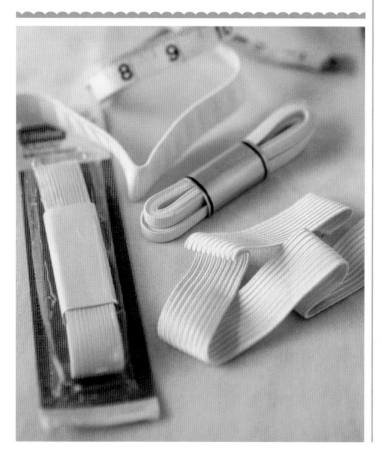

Replacing Elastic Stitched to a Waistband

Some clothing becomes more comfortable with age, like my favorite pair of pj bottoms. Unfortunately, as the fabric softens up, sometimes the elastic starts to give out. The kind of elastic used on exercise pants and boxers is usually stitched right to the fabric waistband. The elastic is easy enough to replace; just follow these steps to keep those favorite pj's fitting just like new.

Step 1. Release the old elastic from the garment by taking out stitches with a seam ripper, being careful not to snag the fabric.

Step 2. Choose new elastic that is the same size and type as the one you removed. Wrap it around your waist and pull it snugly — but not too tight. Add ½" for overlap, and cut.

Step 3. Divide the waist of the garment into four quarters and pin at those four points onto the back center, side seams, and front center.

Step 4. Sew along the bottom edge of the elastic with a zig-zag or overlock stitch (see page 53), stretching the elastic as you work so the fabric is gathered when the elastic returns to its relaxed position.

Step 5. When you get back to the beginning, work a second row of stitching along the top edge of the elastic.

Step 6. To finish the raw elastic edges, simply stitch over them with a zigzag stitch by machine, or overlock stitch if hand-sewing.

Replacing Elastic in a Casing

Step 1. Rip out about 1" of stitching from the casing at a side seam so the repair work isn't noticeable.

Step 2. Cut the old elastic (if not already broken) and pull it out.

Step 3. Choose new elastic that is the same size and type as the one you removed. Wrap it around your waist and pull it snugly-but not too tight. Add 1" for overlap, and cut.

Step 4. Attach a safety pin to one end of the elastic and feed it back through the casing. Don't let the other end of the elastic slip into the casing or you will have to start over.

Step 5. Once the pinned end of the elastic comes back out of the opening, overlap and pin the ends together, being careful not to twist the elastic. Stitch them with a zigzag stitch on the sewing machine or a backstitch by hand.

Step 6. Guide the stitched ends back into the opening and restitch the casing seam using a straight stitch on the machine or a ladder stitch by hand (see page 52).

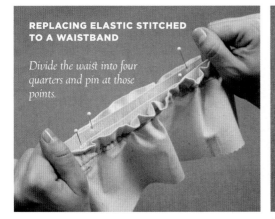

REPLACING ELASTIC STITCHED TO A WAISTBAND

Divide the waist into four quarters and pin at those points.

REPLACING ELASTIC IN A CASING

Thread elastic through casing with a safety pin.

Gathering Repairs

Gathers are a design feature that joins a bigger length of fabric to a smaller one, creating shape and tiny folds of fabric (without elastic). When the stitching that formed the gathers comes loose, the seam opens and the gathers come undone. I like to use hand stitching for this simple fix unless the whole seam needs repair, in which case there is a lot of stitching, so the machine is better up to the task.

REGATHERING FABRIC AT THE WAIST

INSERTING GATHERED FABRIC INTO SEAM OPENING

Step 1. Trim any loose threads and rip out the seam a few inches on each side of the area where the gathers have come undone.

Step 2. Knot your thread and work a long running stitch along the seamline at the repair area. Pull gently on the thread to cinch up the fabric and regather it. Fasten off the thread so the gather stays put.

Step 3. Insert the newly gathered fabric into the seam opening (if necessary open up the seam a bit more) and pin it in place. Adjust the gathers if necessary to make them even.

Step 4. Restitch the seam with a straight stitch by machine or a backstitch by hand. Be sure to backstitch a few stitches on both sides of the repair.

Drawstring Repairs

Many of our everyday clothes have drawstrings: hooded sweatshirts, skirts, and yoga pants. Unfortunately, it's a common occurrence for the drawstrings to pull out in the wash, or disappear in the dryer. Replacing your drawstring is a simple task and it makes a world of a difference because it gives your garment its utility back.

Fixing a Drawstring Hole

The ends of drawstrings are often knotted or made double-thickness to keep them from working their way into the casing and getting lost in your waistband, where they do no good at all. If the hole becomes stretched out or tears, that very thing will happen. Here's a quick fix.

Step 1. Trim any excess threads. Secure your thread to an undamaged area. Hold the drawstring off to the side.

Step 2. Use the buttonhole stitch (see page 52) to work your way around the drawstring hole, being careful *not* to pick up the other side of the fabric with your sewing needle. (That will close the hole, whoops.)

Step 3. Fasten off the thread and you are all set.

Use the buttonhole stitch to repair the drawstring hole.

Making a New Drawstring

I'm not exactly sure how it happens, but from time to time, my drawstrings get lost. Just gone. What to do? I make a new one, thank you. It's really easy, and here's how.

Step 1. Pick out some grosgrain ribbon or twill tape. Cut a piece that's at least 8" longer than the channel you will be feeding it through.

Step 2. Fold the raw ends onto themselves and stitch through the fold with several backstitches (or tie a double knot at each end once it's back in its channel). Or use a little Fray Check on the ends to finish. And that's it. Like I said, easy. Now all you have to do is get it back in the channel (see the next page).

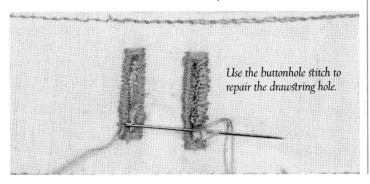

Fold the raw ends of the drawstring and stitch to secure.

Replacing a Drawstring

If your drawstring comes out of its channel, all you need to put it back in place is a safety pin and a little patience.

Step 1. Knot one end of the drawstring and then secure a safety pin to the other, unknotted end.

Step 2. Feed the safety pin into the drawstring hole and push it, along with the drawstring, through the channel. The safety pin gives you something to grip onto.

Step 3. Once you get to the other hole, pull the drawstring end through and remove the safety pin.

Step 4. Knot the end of the drawstring so it won't slip back into the hole.

DRAWSTRING TIPS

➻ Check around the drawstring holes for damage. If they are stretched or torn, it's a good idea to go ahead and mend those as well.

➻ Grosgrain ribbon makes a great drawstring. All you have to do is finish the ends so they don't unravel.

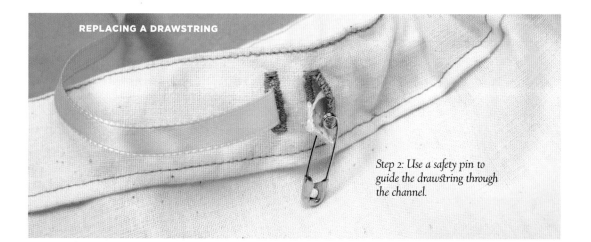

REPLACING A DRAWSTRING

Step 2: Use a safety pin to guide the drawstring through the channel.

Belt Loop Repair

While broken and snapped belt loops have never been a problem for me, they are for my partner. So by proximity, it's my problem because I mend his clothing for him. A torn belt loop is an easy fix, but if you don't do a combination of reinforcing along with reattaching, it will come undone pretty quickly. If it wasn't strong enough to hold up to stress in the first place, it will probably break again without strong stitching.

Making a New Belt Loop

For belt loops, it's very important to make a new one that resembles, as closely as possible, the original. This isn't for fashion reasons, but durability. For instance, don't use calico cotton or other lightweight fabrics in place of denim or khaki. Heavyweight fabrics are great to use for most belt loops because they can stand up to all the strain of keeping your pants around your waist.

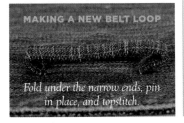

Fold under the narrow ends, pin in place, and topstitch.

Step 1. If the old belt loop is still more or less intact, use it as a template for a new belt loop. Remove all the stitches from the old belt loop and iron it flat. Cut your new belt loop from your new fabric. If you don't have the old belt loop, or it's not usable as a template, cut a 1½" × 3" piece of fabric.

Step 2. Fold the fabric in half lengthwise with wrong sides together, and then fold under the raw edges. Press the belt loop and edgestitch along the long edges. Fold under the narrow ends and pin them in place on the garment. Keep the loop loose so the belt will fit through, and refer to the other belt loops for positioning.

Step 3. Topstitch across the narrow ends to secure the belt loop to the waistband. If hand stitching, use a backstitch.

Reinforcing a Belt Loop

Step 1. Sometimes you need to reinforce the fabric where the belt loop is attached. If it's holding on by a few threads, remove the belt loop so you can patch the fabric using one of the patching techniques in chapter 4.

Step 2. Once the area is patched, pin the belt loop in place and stitch it securely, using a straight stitch on the sewing machine or a backstitch if working by hand. Make several rows or a square of stitches at the top and at the bottom of the loop. And that should do it.

Release from the torn area, patch, and stitch to the patched fabric.

WHAT A MESS DRESS

by Marisa Lynch

Never say "toss it" if something gets spotted, tears, or loses a few buttons. And in this case, a few buttons meant all of them! This dress came out of a big pile of toss-aways and was snagged for just a dollar. Usually, a garment with torn seams would be enough for most people to pass right by, but when you add no buttons to the equation, it's a no-brainer. It's not going to work, or is it? The color palette and fabric design of this dress made me do a double take when I first saw it. After a little inspection, I decided to take it home with me and attempt to restore it from its unwearable state. Here's how I did it.

➻ First, I went on a button search. After searching through a blue/green color palette, I chose a forest green shade in the perfect round shape and size to fit the existing buttonholes.

➻ With needle and thread, I hand-sewed each of the six buttons in place. Luckily there were thread remnants in the spaces where the original buttons once were, making great guides to where the new ones should go.

➻ There were a few other snafus that needed to be handled, including multiple tears underneath the sleeves and armpits. Not so cute. I pinned the openings at the seams, got my sewing machine set up, and stitched up the gaps. No more underarm breezes!

➻ With just a little sleeve rolling, a belt or a vintage pin at the back to adjust the fit, and some ballet flats, this dress turned out fabulous! Who would have thought a buttonless, torn dress would look so put together?

I took this picture of the dress before I repaired it.

Darning

I love darning. I can easily say that it is my absolute favorite mending method. While working by hand takes a little more time, I love the way it looks. I love the process of stitching and weaving my clothing back to a state of wearability. And better yet, I love the way it holds up over time.

So, What Is Darning?

Essentially, instead of taking a piece of fabric and stitching it to the damaged area to replace what's missing, you knit, crochet, or weave fabric threads directly into the damaged fabric. The first part of the process involves stitching a series of rows around the damaged area to prevent the fabric from fraying further. Then you weave or knit extra threads through the fabric.

Woven darning is by far the easiest, but don't let that deter you from attempting the knitted or crocheted methods. It just takes a little more practice. Though it's now my favorite, darning was the last mending technique I learned.

me out a little too much. In a pinch, I use an Easter egg, but wooden eggs from the craft store make the best darning eggs. Check out page 126 for how to make your own darning egg, and below for sourcing different types of darning eggs new and old.

What the Heck Is a Darning Egg?

Essentially, a darning egg is just an egg-shaped surface to support cloth while you are working on it. The egg shape provides just the right curve to maintain the size and shape of the hole or damaged area. Some people say they use lightbulbs, but that just freaks

SEARCHING FOR AN ANTIQUE

Usually people do not know a darning egg when they see one, so you might be able to get this gem for cheap if you happen to find one. Antique shops, on the other hand, usually know what they are, and charge anywhere from $35 to $400 depending on its condition, age, the material it is made out of, and if it has any special historical significance, such as a Shaker darning tool. If you just want one and the cost doesn't matter, eBay will give you the instant gratification you need. There are usually quite a few available for auction, ranging in price from $10 to $200.

Knit vs. Woven

Before you start darning, identify whether the fabric you're working with is knit or woven. Here's how you tell them apart.

KNIT FABRICS

Knit Fabric: Loops in Loops

Knit fabric is a series of interlocking loops; it can be as bulky as sweater fabric or as fine as the fabric used for T-shirts. When a knit fabric tears, the interlocking loops start to unravel. One loop slips out of the loop above it and the loops continue to slip and come unstitched until they are stopped, either by you or the edge of the sweater.

Woven Fabric: Warp and Weft

Woven fabrics are created on a loom, with lengthwise (warp) and crosswise (weft) threads. The weft threads are woven over and under the warp threads in different patterns depending on the desired weave. The threads are then "combed" into place with a reed that keeps the threads straight and compact. The plain weave is the most common weave, with a consistent "one over, one under" pattern. Twill weaves with their distinctive diagonal lines produce strong and durable fabrics that are often used to make pants. Satin weave fabrics have a smooth surface because the warp yarns float over several weft yarns; they tend to unravel more than the other two weaves. All woven fabrics have a selvage, or finished edge, along the outside edges of the warp yarns.

TWILL FABRICS

PLAIN WOVEN

Darning by Machine

*M*ost *darning is done by hand,* but if you don't care whether the mending is visible, you can darn by machine. It can really look neat by using a brightly colored thread. You'll need to sew without the presser foot or use a darning foot with the feed dogs lowered so that you can manipulate the fabric under the needle in side-to-side and back-and-forth motions. Many machines have a darning setting that uses the buttonhole foot, but you can also use a small straight stitch (as pictured below); refer to your owner's manual for setting instructions specific to your machine. What does that darning stitch look like on your machine? The stitch is usually represented by an icon that looks like a small grid. By having a series of small stitches worked closely together vertically and then horizontally, all the loose ends get locked down. Machine mending usually works best on flat pieces versus things like sock heels.

Step 1. Cut a piece of lightweight interfacing that is larger than the frayed area and apply it to the wrong side of the fabric.

Step 2. Sew a square around the area to be darned with the straight stitch; catch the interfacing in the stitching.

Step 3. Switch your sewing machine to the darning stitch setting, or if you don't have a darning setting, you can use a straight stitch.

Step 4. Follow the steps in your sewing machine's manual to complete the darning or stitch back and forth horizontally, then vertically, working the rows 1/16" apart.

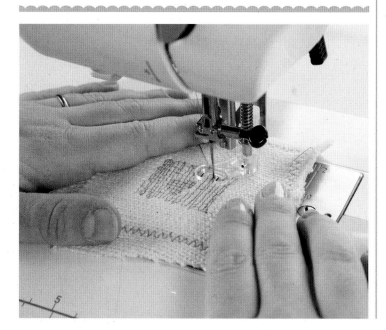

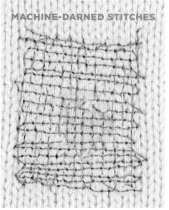

MACHINE-DARNED STITCHES

Darning by Hand

f the damaged area is small, you can mend it with thread; but if it is a large hole or tear, you should secure a fabric or interfacing patch on the wrong side and darn over the patch for greater durability and to make the mending job quicker.

For Woven and Knit Fabrics

Step 1. Secure your thread by working several stitches in an undamaged part of the cloth.

Step 2. Work a running stitch around the damaged area a couple of times. Why? Well, you want to make sure that the hole doesn't unravel anymore. Working several stitches around the damaged area will help to lock the stitches into place.

Step 3. Work several straight stitches across the opening, starting and ending the stitches close to the running stitches. This creates a cluster of parallel threads to then weave a second series of stitches through.

Step 4. Work a series of stitches perpendicular to the parallel rows, weaving the threads over and under the parallel threads in the desired pattern.

Step 5. To fasten off, don't knot the thread; instead weave the ends in the stitches.

Swiss Darning Knit Fabrics

Swiss darning, also called the duplicate stitch, is really great for mending areas that haven't busted through completely. You trace the knit stitches by following the pattern of the underlying stitches.

Step 1. Start tracing stitches in an undamaged part of the cloth, close to the damaged area, by working several stitches in and out of the fabric.

Step 2. With the knit side of fabric facing you, insert the needle behind the two vertical bars of the knit loop directly

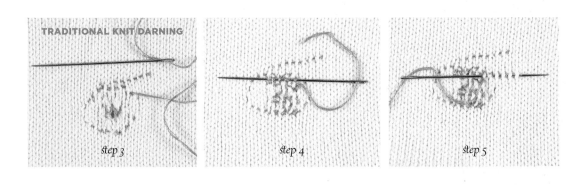

TRADITIONAL KNIT DARNING

step 3   *step 4*   *step 5*

above the loop you want to trace and pull the yarn through.

Step 3. Reinsert the needle behind the two vertical bars of the knit loop directly below the loop you want to trace and pull the yarn through.

Step 4. Continue catching two vertical bars above and then below, which will cause the needle to be inserted twice in each loop. Continue until you have traced, or covered, all the worn or tired stitches.

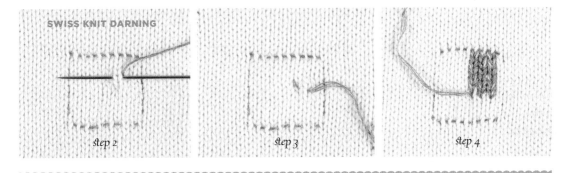

SWISS KNIT DARNING

step 2

step 3

step 4

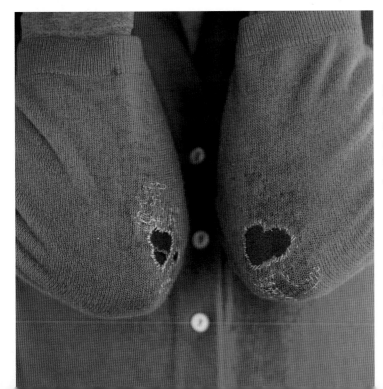

DARNED ELBOWS

I used old T-shirt fabric to create a support for woven darning and embroidery in this favorite sweater. With knit fabric, it's easy to shape the holes into hearts, for a loving touch.

MAKE YOUR OWN DARNING EGG

by Kristin Roach

While working on this book, I looked all around central Iowa for a darning egg. It turns out that they are very difficult to find. You can't just go to your local craft shop and pick one up, and even in the antique shops they can be pretty hard to locate. If you are lucky, you may just find one at a thrift store, but estate sales seem to be the best place.

Here's another option that you may want to try: making your own. With a quick trip to the wood craft section of your local craft supply store, you can get most of what you need for about $5. The general idea is to drill a hole in the wooden sphere, which you then fill with glue and a shaker peg. Once you make the basic form, you can paint or decorate it any way you wish. It's a pretty fun and easy project.

What You'll Need

1 shaker peg

1 wooden egg or sphere

Wood glue

Cotton swab

Bench clamp

Drill and a bit to fit peg end (see step 2)

Paint, glitter, markers, and so on (optional)

Acrylic varnish and brushes

What You'll Do

Step 1. Mark the general center at the base of the egg.

Step 2. Clamp the egg into the bench clamp and drill a hole ½" deep (or the depth of the peg end).

Step 3. Use a cotton swab to dab wood glue inside the hole. Put some more glue onto the tenon end of the peg.

Step 4. Insert the tenon into the hole and set it aside. Do not disturb it for at least 30 minutes so it has time to set up a bit.

Step 5. Decorate the egg with paint, glitter, charcoal, markers, or anything you see fit. Or just use a simple stain or coat of paint. Seal it with an acrylic varnish. Let the darning egg dry by tying a string around the peg and hanging it from a hook, the rafters in the garage, or some place where it will not rest against anything.

NOTE: *These instructions are for making one egg, but you might want to make extra as gifts for friends. I used pegs about 3" long with a ⅜" tenon (a woodworking term for the peg end you insert into the egg).*

DARN-IT-ALL CROCHET

by Cal Patch

There's more than one way to darn a hole, that's for sure. The traditional method involves a sort of cross between embroidering and weaving. That way works fine, but as a fan of crochet, I've always felt that using crochet to patch worn areas makes more sense for a bunch of reasons:

- ●▸ Crochet is stretchy, whereas weaving is not.
- ●▸ Crochet creates a sturdy, double-thickness fabric, which will hold up even better than the original.
- ●▸ Crochet has an inherent ability to be shaped and molded to fit any kind of hole.

I won't even get into how pretty it is, or how many fancy stitch possibilities there are to play with. But for socks without heels, or worn-out elbows, you'll probably want to keep it simple and use the trusty old single crochet stitch. These areas get a lot of wear and are likely to need mending again if you choose a delicate, lacy pattern. What follows is my basic technique that I've used on knit sweaters and socks, T-shirts, and even woven garments.

What You'll Need

Yarn that's comparable in weight and fiber content to the piece you are repairing (unless, like me, you prefer an extra-heavy heel cushion)

A fine crochet hook for getting started

Another hook suitable to the size of yarn you'll be working with

A tapestry needle

Scissors

What You'll Do

Step 1. Use small, sharp scissors to cut away the worn and fraying edges of the hole. Also trim away any thread runs because they will only continue to spread. It's better to trim enough so that you'll only be crocheting into good strong fabric. If you work into worn fabric, the patch will soon tear away.

Step 2. Using your tiniest crochet hook (you don't want to tear any stitches of the surrounding fabric when you poke the hook into it), join your yarn to the edge of the hole with a slip stitch. See following page for diagrams on how to start a slip stitch.

Step 3. Work single crochet stitches around the circumference of the hole (see Crochet School on page 131), keeping the stitches close together to enclose the cut edge.

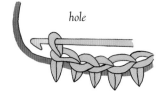

hole

Step 4. At the end of the first row, join the yarn to the first stitch with another slip stitch, and switch to a bigger hook if you want to.

Step 5. Continue to fill in the hole with consecutive rounds of single crochet, decreasing as necessary. (To decrease, insert your hook into the next *two* stitches instead of one.) In this case, I guesstimated that I would need six or seven more rounds to fill in the hole, so I began by decreasing every sixth stitch in the next round, and decreased more frequently as I progressed to the smaller rounds. When I got to the last two rounds, I decreased every stitch, and then finished off, leaving a long tail.

STARTING A SLIP STITCH

Pull a loop through the fabric.

Wrap the yarn over the hook.

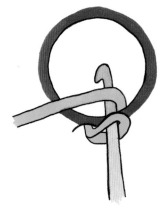

Pull the yarn through the first loop.

→ For a sock heel, work two full rounds before you start decreasing.

→ When darning a flat hole, begin decreasing on the second round.

Step 6. Thread the yarn tail onto a tapestry needle and, from the wrong side, sew the hole closed and weave in the end of the yarn. On flat pieces, a quick steaming with the iron can make everything lie smoothly, especially if you've crocheted with wool yarn.

Crocheted darning is a great way to use remnants of yarn skeins.

CROCHET SCHOOL

If you don't know how to crochet, don't fret. Here are the basic steps (shown on a practice chain of stitches, but the principle is the same).

Step 1. Begin the first row of single crochet by inserting the hook through the second chain from the hook.

Step 2. Bring the yarn over the hook from the back to the front.

Step 3. Pull the yarn to the front and move it to the shank of the hook. There are now two loops on the hook.

Step 4. Bring the yarn over the hook again from back to front and pull it through both loops on the hook.

Step 5. You now have one loop on the hook and have completed one single crochet.

WOVEN STAR DARNING

by Diane Gilleland

Sure, a patch can work well to cover up a hole, but sometimes you want something a little more decorative. This technique is based on the traditional darning method used to repair knit garments, but we've used it to create a sturdy woven patch on the surface of the fabric. The same process can be used to darn a hole in any knit (starting at step 4), but use matching thread for a less obvious finish.

What You'll Need

Embroidery hoop

Water-soluble fabric marker

Crewel needle with a large eye and sharp point

Pearl cotton embroidery floss*

Scissors

Lightweight fusible interfacing and iron

* It's best to use only colorfast floss for this and any project. To test your floss, fill a small bowl with warm, soapy water. Soak a strand of floss in it for about 10 minutes. Rinse it in clean water, press out excess moisture, and lay it on paper towels to dry. If any dye ends up on the paper towel, the floss is not colorfast.

Preparing the Garment

Step 1. Cut a piece of fusible interfacing about 1" larger on all sides than the shape you plan to weave. Follow the manufacturer's instructions to fuse it to the wrong side of the garment, under the spot where you'll be weaving.

Step 2. Draw an outline of the shape you want to weave onto the outside of the garment, using a water-soluble fabric marker. You can draw freehand, or cut a shape from card stock and trace it onto the garment. If your garment is dark-colored, you may prefer to use tailor's chalk, so the lines are more easily visible.

Step 3. Place this section of your garment into an embroidery hoop. Stretch it as taut as possible. Try to place the hoop in a place on the fabric so it doesn't catch any buttons, zippers, or bulky seams, all of which will cause the fabric to sag in the hoop.

Stitching the Warp Threads

Step 4. Thread a needle with about 24" of embroidery floss. Tie a secure knot in one end.

Step 5. Starting in the center of the shape, bring the needle up from the wrong side on one of the marked (or stitched) lines. Pull the floss through and insert the needle back down straight across the shape

on the opposite marked line. This long stitch is the first "warp" thread for your weaving, and it will be the guide for the rest of the warp threads.

Step 6. Continue making stitches on each side of the first one, keeping them parallel and spacing them about ⅛" apart. The ends of these stitches should follow the outline of the shape that you traced, stitched, or drew. Keep these stitches pulled taut. If your shape is complex, you may need to place some shorter warp stitches in portions of the design. Just follow your outline and add stitches where needed to fill it in.

Step 7. When you've finished the warp stitching, knot the floss securely on the inside of the garment.

Weaving the Weft Threads

Step 8. Thread a 36" strand of floss onto your needle, and tie a secure knot in one end.

Step 9. You can begin at the bottom or top of your shape — whichever offers the simplest contours. Bring the needle up just outside one of the outer warp stitches.

Step 10. Carefully weave your needle under and over the warp stitches, pulling the floss along, until you have woven your way across the shape. Pull any excess floss through and gently slide it so it rests neatly along the edge of the shape. Pass the needle back down through the garment just outside the outermost warp to tack the woven piece to the garment.

Step 11. Bring the needle back up close to the end of the previous row of weaving.

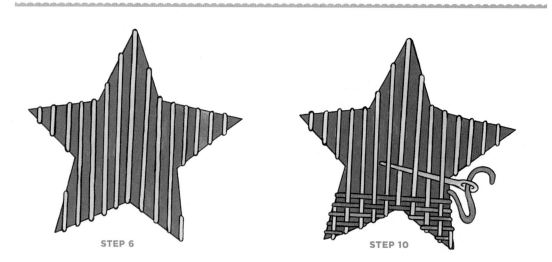

STEP 6   STEP 10

Then, weave the needle over and under the warp threads, this time, weaving them opposite to the previous row. (Meaning, if you passed under a warp stitch in the previous row, you'll pass over it in this row.) When you've woven your way across the row, pull the floss through and adjust it so it lies smoothly against the first row. Then, pass the needle down through the garment at the end of the row.

Step 12. Repeat step 11 until you've filled in the entire shape with weaving, following the traced (or drawn or stitched) outlines. Knot the floss securely on the inside of the garment.

Finishing the Garment

Step 13. Remove the embroidery hoop. You may wish to fuse another layer of interfacing over the back of your stitches to smooth them and seal them in.

Step 14. As a finishing touch, you can also embroider around the edge of the shape with backstitches (see page 50).

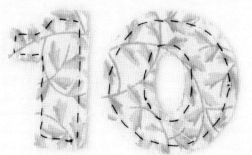

Fasteners and Closures

Fasteners come in all shapes and sizes. From the littlest of snaps to the biggest of buttons, these pieces are the greatest points of stress in your clothing. Buttonholes will stretch out and quit holding buttons. Clasps, hooks, and snaps will wear out. In all the mending I've ever done, sewing buttons back on and replacing those little hooks at the top of zippers are the most common tasks.

Buttons and Buttonholes

Buttons come in all shapes and sizes and it can be a real problem when one pops off your favorite shirt. Well, how about keeping them from popping off in the first place? When you buy clothing from the store, the buttons are sewn on by machine and aren't usually fastened very well, if at all. I know, I know, this sounds like a real pain, but if you buy a shirt because the buttons caught your eye just as much as the fabric and style, grab a needle and thread and tack those babies down securely.

First things first: How do you sew a button on to begin with? All you need is a needle, thread, and some scissors. Oh, and of course the button. What kind of button do you have? And what's the difference anyway? There are two basic types of buttons, those with a shank and those without.

SHANK BUTTONS

Shank Buttons

A shank, located on the back of a button, is a little loop of metal or a plastic bump with a hole in it. The shank lifts the button off the garment and provides a hole for the thread. Shank buttons are traditionally pretty fancy and are often made out of glass, bronze, and even gold.

Did you know that originally buttons didn't actually fasten anything at all? At first they were purely for decoration. When buttonholes were first invented — kind of crazy to think that even buttonholes had to be invented — they were so popular that aristocrats wore clothing with rows and rows of buttons and buttonholes that matched up perfectly. Can you imagine having to sew a coat with 100 buttons and 100 corresponding buttonholes? Freaking excessive!

Thank goodness when it comes to mending we are dealing with far fewer buttons and lining them up with buttonholes that already exist.

Step 1. Close the garment and make a mark through the center of the buttonhole to indicate where the button should go.

Step 2. Secure a double length thread at the back of the work with a knot.

Step 3. Work several stitches through the shank and the garment.

Step 4. Bring the needle and thread to the right side of the garment and wrap the thread around the shank a few times.

Step 5. Bring the needle to the back of the work and fasten off the thread with a double loop knot (see page 47).

Shankless Buttons

You can sew on a shankless (sew-through) button so it lies flat against the fabric, which is okay for lightweight fabrics and buttons that are decorative.

Step 1. Close the garment and make a mark through the center of the buttonhole to indicate where the button should go.

Step 2. Secure a double length thread at the back of the work with a knot and bring it to the right side of the garment through one of the button's holes. Bring the thread back down through the opposite hole and the fabric. Repeat several times and through all the holes.

Step 3. Bring the needle to the back of the work and fasten off the thread with a double loop knot (see page 47).

Making a Shank for a Shankless Button

Sometimes you need to create your own shank when sewing on a flat button. It's particularly smart when sewing buttons on jackets or to any thick material. It's easy to do with the help of two straight pins, a sewing needle, and thread. This method creates a thread

SHANKLESS BUTTONS

shank so the button stands away from the fabric slightly.

Step 1. Close the garment and make a mark through the center of the buttonhole to indicate where the button should go. Insert and cross two straight pins at the button location.

Step 2. Secure a double length thread at the back of the work with a knot and bring it to the right side of the garment through one of the button's holes. Bring the thread back down through the opposite hole and the fabric. Repeat several times and through all the holes in the button.

Step 3. Remove the pins and wrap the thread around the thread that extends from the button to the fabric three or four times.

Step 4. Bring the needle to the back of the work and fasten off the thread with a double loop knot (see page 47).

Reinforcing the Fabric Behind Buttons

Sometimes the problem is that the fabric behind the buttons is giving out. This is an easy fix.

Step 1. Trim any excess threads. If there is a hole that's worn through under the button, but the button is still attached, go ahead and remove the button.

Step 2. Attach a small patch of fabric or an iron-on patch to the back of the fabric (see page 62).

Step 3. Reattach the button.

Fixing Frayed Buttonholes

Buttonholes become stretched out and frayed over time. A very easy way to repair them is to restitch them.

Step 1. Trim any loose threads and secure the new thread to the underside of the fabric with a few backstitches.

Step 2. Use the buttonhole stitch (see page 50) to restitch the buttonhole edges. If one part of the buttonhole is particularly stretched out, work a running stitch all the way around the edge of the buttonhole before working the buttonhole stitch.

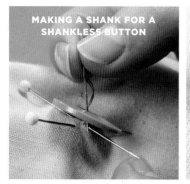
MAKING A SHANK FOR A SHANKLESS BUTTON

REINFORCING FABRIC BEHIND A BUTTON

FIXING A FRAYED BUTTONHOLE

Sew-On Hooks and Eyes

*H*ooks are used to help support other fasteners. They are commonly found at the top of zippers and help the zipper stay closed by keeping the top edges of the garment together. On pants and skirts, they are often used to give the waistband a finished look.

Unfortunately these little helpers often fall off and are never replaced. What's the harm if you barely notice it's gone? Here's the problem: because the hook (or sew-on snap) is missing there is unneeded stress on the button or zipper it was supposed to help. Before you know it, your zipper could jam, eat up fabric, or come unzipped at inopportune times, and your buttons might start popping right off. Do yourself a favor and take five minutes to stitch these fasteners back on.

Replacing Eye Hooks

When I first started mending, I attached my hooks across the base of the hook, treating each loop as a buttonhole. This did absolutely nothing for providing stability to the hook and was ineffective for keeping the fabric together. It was only last year when I realized the error of my ways. Once you've chosen a replacement hook and eye, here's what you do.

Step 1. Secure a double length thread with a knot at the hook location, taking care that the stitches don't show on the right side.

Step 2. Sew several small straight stitches around the outer edge of one loop of the hook. Again, take care that stitches don't show on the right side.

Step 3. Bring the needle over and through the other loop and work several stitches around that loop, as in step 2.

Step 4. Bring the needle under and up again at the front of the hook and work several stitches over the stem, just under the shaped part of the hook. Fasten off the thread.

Step 5. Attaching the eye that complements the hook is just as simple. Secure the thread to the fabric at the location of the eye and work several stitches around both of the loops as in step 2.

Step 6. Fasten off the thread as in step 4. You are all set.

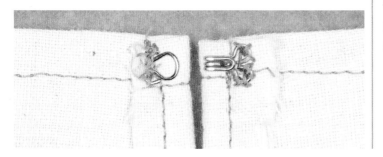

It's a Snap

*T*here are two kinds of snaps: decorative snaps that require an application tool and sew-on snaps that are used inside garments. If the snaps on your jeans, or even the fancy little snaps on your favorite cowboy shirt, are still attached to the fabric, try fixing them before completely replacing them with sew-on snaps. The reason snaps lose their snap is because they don't fit together like they should. Try to pinch and bend the snaps back to their original shape with needle-nose pliers. If that works, great; you'll have fixed another garment. If it doesn't work, you'll have to remove and replace the snap completely. And when you replace it, use a sew-on snap. Why? Well, a few reasons. One is you don't need any special tools and the other is that the teeth of decorative snaps cause more stress to the fabric than sew-on snaps.

If you have to replace a decorative snap, remove both pieces of the snap completely. Then you'll probably have to patch the area that was underneath the snap, since the teeth of the snap tend to tear the fabric. As long as the decorative snap wasn't integral to the design of the garment, simply secure a sew-on snap to the inside of the garment.

Attaching Sew-On Snaps

Step 1. Mark the desired location on the garment with your favorite marking tool or two straight pins.

Step 2. Position the ball half of the snap on the garment with the ball facing up. Secure the thread to the wrong side of the fabric with a knot and bring it to the right side next to the snap.

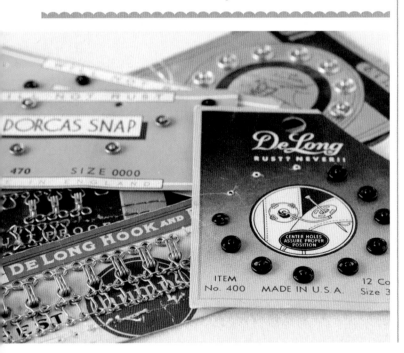

Step 3. Stitch around the perimeter of the snap by drawing the needle through each of the holes three or four times, picking up just a few garment threads so the stitching doesn't show on the garment front.

Step 4. Position the socket half of the snap, with the hollow part facing up, on the garment after aligning it with the ball half. Secure the thread to the wrong side of the fabric with a knot and bring it to the right side next to the snap. Sew the socket in place.

BUTTON IT UP!

I received this handmade shirt as a hand-me-down from a neighbor. The clear, plain buttons on it were chipped and outdated. These turquoise buttons add a touch of color and bring out the playful pattern on the vintage fabric.

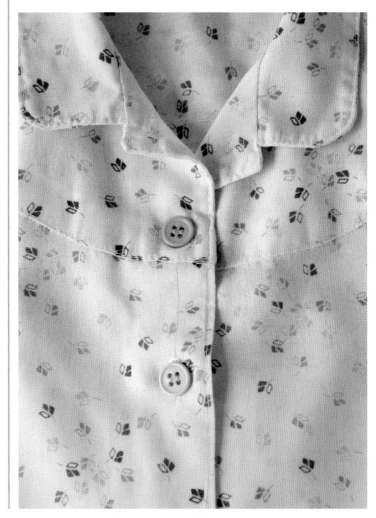

LEATHER CLASPS AND TRIMMINGS

by Francesca Mueller

This is the cardigan I wore when I was pregnant with my daughter. From the early months of my pregnancy in the springtime, right down to the last stages in midwinter, this cardigan was my faithful companion. It eventually felt and looked pretty shapeless and large, and found a home at the bottom of my wardrobe. I never considered getting rid of it, though, not only because I was attached to it, but also because repurposing, mending, and giving new life to our belongings is part of the lifestyle we've chosen for our family.

To become functional again, my overused pregnancy cardigan needed to fit more snugly, and to gain some structure. It would also benefit from some accents, to make it more interesting. In order to pursue all these goals, here is what I did. You can use these same techniques on your own clothing that needs to be updated.

After I had my baby, the cardigan I wore when I was pregnant needed a makeover.

Adding Binding

Step 1. I made bias tape binding to encase the neckline and cuffs. Making your own bias tape binding is a fairly basic sewing technique, and useful for a lot of different mending tasks. You can buy ready-made binding, of course, though it costs a lot more than making it yourself, and you have to be satisfied with the patterns and colors available in the store. The binding I made was ½"-wide double-fold. (*To make your own bias binding, see* Binding Basics *on page* 149)

Step 2. To attach the binding to a pocket or garment edge, insert the edge(s) of the garment between the folds of the bias binding and edgestitch close to the innermost edge of the binding, through all the layers. Nothin' to it! Here's a little trick, though. If you're using ready-made tape, look closely at the edges. You'll see that the folded sides are not exactly the same width. When sewing on ready-made bias tape, position the narrower side on the top of the fabric and the wider side in back, so when you are stitching along

the top, you will automatically catch the back fold with your stitches.

Because wool knits are elastic and can be quite spongy, it is very helpful (when working on tricky fabrics) to baste the tape in place first. This extra step can save a lot of time later since ripping out stitches in knit fabrics is a frustrating job.

Making Fasteners

Step 1. I removed the single button from my sweater, and darned the buttonhole closed (see page 140). My goal was to replace the single button with three new buttons, made from handmade (bias tape) fabric and leather tabs. I moved the button placement away from the finished edge, so that the cardigan fronts would have

more of an overlap and fit more closely.

Step 2. Prepare a length of bias tape in the fabric of your choice (see page 149). To make the bias tape ties, edgestitch the bias tape through both layers, along the folds, creating a flat fabric "string" which you can then use to make three loops and three button knots. Cut the bias tape into three 4" lengths for the loops, and three lengths, about 10" long, for the button knots. Set the 4" lengths aside for the moment.

Step 3. The knot shown is called a Celtic button knot (see page 147). Make three button knots in the center of each 10"-long piece of bias tape (see Tied in Knots). Trim the ends as needed and put the buttons aside for the moment.

— narrower fold

STEP 2 *Positioning the narrower side of the bias tape on top of the fabric ensures you will automatically catch the back fold with your stitches.*

Step 4. Cut six small pieces of leather the same shape as the template provided. Leather (real or faux washable leather) is an excellent material for mending clothes because it's durable, flexible, and doesn't require hemming. You may find that the knit and leather together are too thick and bulky to fit into your sewing machine. If so, simply run the sewing machine over only the leather pieces, without thread, to make holes where you'll later make the stitches. Then you can hand-sew through the ready-made holes.

Step 5. To attach the fasteners, mark the desired location on the sweater with pins. Fold the 4" lengths of bias tape in half to make loops and sandwich the ends between two pieces of leather. Sandwich the ends of the button knots between two pieces of leather as well. Attach the loops and knots to the sweater at the marked locations by hand stitching through the leather, catching the loop and knot ends in the stitching.

CLASP TEMPLATE

TIED IN KNOTS

Button knots are a great way to add a little touch of fancy (made with silk) or casual chic (made with linen or cotton cord) to any garment that's missing its regular buttons. While it's a fairly easy knot to tie, it can be a little tricky cinching it up correctly. You can see here how I have used them, combined with pieces of leather, to make clasps to update my favorite sweater. Use cord (silk, nylon, cotton, or even hemp) or bias binding to make your own button knots.

Step 1. Using a safety pin or a piece of tape, secure one end of your cord to a work surface, like a table or pillow. Make a counterclockwise loop so the end of the cord is on top of the secured end. (See the illustration on the next page.)

Step 2. Make a second loop that overlaps the first and is slightly to the right of it.

Step 3. Take the unsecured end and feed it through the loops working right to left, going over, under, over, under.

Step 4. Bring the cord counterclockwise (left to right) along the bottom of the piece passing over the taped end, feed it back through the loops, including the one just made, going over the first, then under two, over two.

Step 5. Cinch the knot together by pulling on each end of the cord, taking care to avoid excess cord buildup in the knot.

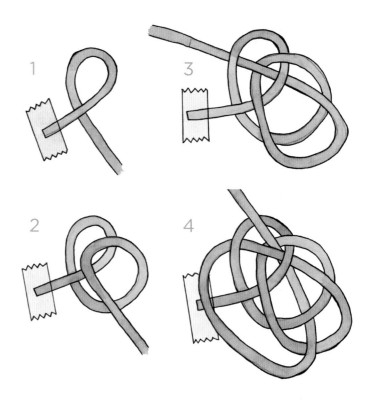

MY FAMILY INSPIRATION

We try to follow in the footsteps of generations before us, our mothers and grandmothers who lived through two world wars, and the elderly farmers who have been our neighbors for the last decade. These people have taught us so much about the value of a simple life with minimal waste, and about the practical skills needed to live it. They've also taught us to enjoy and take pride in something that we've taken the time to make or fix for ourselves.

BINDING BASICS

To make your own bias binding, follow the steps below. These instructions work for making bias binding trimmings, drawstrings or ties:

Step 1. Decide how wide you want your finished bias binding. You will need to cut bias strips of fabric four times the desired finished width. Also decide how much bias binding you need in order to determine how many bias strips to cut. You will probably need to piece the strips together to have the length you need.

Step 2. To find the bias of your fabric, place your fabric wrong side up and align the 45-degree angle line of your quilting ruler along the selvage edge of your fabric. Use your fabric-marking pen to draw a straight line along the edge of your ruler to mark the bias. Draw a line parallel to the first line the desired finished width away. For example, your lines would be 2" apart to create ½" bias tape. Cut enough strips as needed to make enough bias binding for your project.

Step 3. With the right sides together, stitch the two short ends together to make one long strip. Press the seam open. Continue stitching the pieces together to obtain the length you need.

Step 4. With the wrong sides together, fold the bias strip in half lengthwise, aligning the raw edges, and press.

Step 5. Open the strip and press the raw edges on both sides in to the crease. (If you want finished ends for a belt or tie, press both short ends under ½".)

Step 6. Refold along the original fold line and press.

Step 7. Use the bias tape to bind the edges of a project, or edgestitch it closed and use it as a belt, drawstring, or tie.

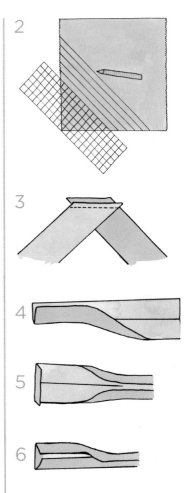

NOTE: *Looking for a shortcut? There is a great tool called a bias tape maker that simplifies folding the edges of the tape. You can find it in fabric stores or online in different widths.*

FABRIC-COVERED BUTTONS

by Kristin Roach

Fabric-covered buttons make beautiful accents on any garment. You can make them from silk, wool, cotton, or just about any woven fabric, since each type of fabric lends its own special touch. I especially like using fabric-covered buttons to dress up accessories and to update jackets and sweaters. Originally, it was only peasants that used such buttons. Aristocrats had metal and glass buttons, while commoners made their buttons from scraps of old cloth. In some territories, it was actually illegal to have fancy buttons on your clothes unless you were of a certain social stature. Thank goodness that is no longer the case!

What You'll Need

Button kit

Scraps of fabric cut into circles

What You'll Do

Step 1. Cut the fabric to the size specified by the template that comes with the button kit.

Step 2. Center the fabric with the wrong side up over the rubber mold and push the button shell into the mold along with the fabric.

Step 3. Tuck the edges of the fabric over the button shell and place the button back over the fabric edges.

Step 4. Place the pusher into the button back and push firmly into the mold. Presto change-o, you now have a fabric-covered button. Make as many as you need for your project.

pusher

button back

button shell

fabric

mold

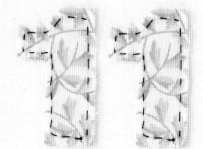

Zippers

Considering how much I like mending, it's funny how long it took me to replace the zipper on my favorite messenger bag. It is a very simple bag and there is only one secure pocket on it. Of course that led to maxing out its carrying capacity for several years. When the pocket started to fail, just a little gap by the top zipper tab, I let it slide. Which is so ridiculous, because if I had just taken the time to fix it then, I may have avoided a total refit. In this chapter, I will show you a few ways to fix your zippers when they need your attention.

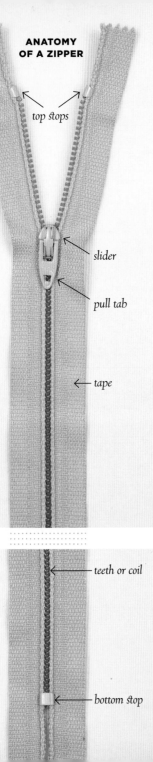

ANATOMY OF A ZIPPER

- top stops
- slider
- pull tab
- tape
- teeth or coil
- bottom stop

Zippers 101

How do you keep your zippers working? Zippers are strong, and with a little preventative care, they usually outlast the garment. Here are some pointers for care and maintenance:

❧ Keep them closed when you store and wash them.

❧ Repair loose stitching as soon as you notice it.

❧ When pressing your clothing, don't apply direct heat to the zippers. It damages them, especially the plastic ones.

❧ Make sure to push aside the fabric when closing and opening the zipper so the cloth doesn't jam up the teeth.

How might a zipper fail? Let me count the ways!

CAUGHT THREADS

Caught threads: Trim any threads caught in the zipper teeth or coil as much as you can and slowly work the zipper down. Pick out the cut threads. Never force a zipper up, because it might become misaligned. If there are loose threads still around the zipper, tack them down with a few stitches or a spot of seam sealant.

Sticky zipper: Like all metal working parts, zippers sometimes need a little help moving smoothly. Beeswax, candle wax, or my great-aunt's favorite, a bar of soap, will usually get things sliding nicely. Just rub the lubricant on the teeth of the zipper to help loosen things up.

Missing teeth: If a tooth is missing in a separating zipper or near the top of a nonseparating zipper, you will need to replace the whole zipper. But if teeth are missing toward the bottom of the nonseparating zipper, you can bypass the problem. Position the pull tab above the broken teeth and with a heavy-duty thread, work several straight stitches across the teeth right above the missing ones. This makes a new bottom stop so you can still use the zipper; you just won't be able to unzip it all the way.

Caught fabric: Just as with the caught threads, do not force the zipper up or down if fabric is caught in it. Instead, work the fabric out of the slider by moving the slider slightly as you very gently manipulate the edge of the fabric. If you can't get it out, you may need to remove the zipper slider with a pair of needle-nose pliers. Replacing the whole zipper

will be easier than trying to fix a torn lining or worse, outer garment edge.

Misaligned Zipper

My poor messenger bag has needed almost every type of mending, including a variety of zipper repairs. The slider was too loose, which caused the teeth to misalign. I had to remove the stop, reset the zipper teeth, and then tweak the slider so it would actually pull things together properly. Trying easy fixes on a zipper takes less than 15 minutes and you have nothing to lose, so don't be intimidated by these useful closures.

Broken slider: You can purchase new zipper sliders from most craft shops. The slider kit will include a new slider and

stop. Replace the broken slider by removing the top stops with a pair of needle-nose pliers. Unzip the broken slider right off the teeth and set it aside. Place the two rows of zipper teeth at the openings of the new slider and feed them in, holding them together. Work the slider up and down several times, making sure the teeth are aligned properly. Attach the new stop(s) provided, or stitch new ones using a heavy-duty thread, just like you would if you were shortening a zipper.

Zipper separates in the middle or top: This usually happens when the zipper slider is too loose. Squeeze the slider as shown with a pair of pliers on one side of the pull tab and then on the other, applying even pressure.

MISSING TEETH

CAUGHT FABRIC

LOOSE SLIDER

Squeeze with pliers to tighten.

Replacing Zippers

If you've already repaired the same zipper a time or two, it's probably best to go ahead and replace it. Here's a tip for attaching any zipper. When I was first learning to sew, it was a revolutionary idea for me to stop stitching, lift up the presser foot, and unzip the zipper so I could sew more easily around the slider and zipper pull. It's so simple and it makes so much sense, but it eluded me until I was in my early twenties. Here's a list of the most common kinds of zippers and how to repair each one.

Centered Zippers

Usually sewn into the backs of skirts, shirts, and dresses, centered zippers form a neat closure on both garments and home décor items.

Step 1. Before ripping out the zipper, mark the original zipper stitching lines on the right side of the garment with tailor's chalk and a ruler as a guide.

Step 2. Free the zipper from the garment by removing all the stitches around the zipper. I like to use a seam ripper. If your zipper top is sewn into a waistband or collar, you need to remove a few of the stitches at the waistband or collar seam. You will have to restitch the seam once the new zipper is in place.

Step 3. Baste the zipper opening closed and press the seam flat. With the wrong side of your work facing you, place the new zipper right side down, and align the closed zipper teeth with the basted seam. Temporarily secure the zipper in place with basting stitches, dressmaker pins, or basting tape; you don't want it slipping around while you are trying to stitch it nice and neatly. Once basted in place, remove the center basting.

Step 4. Thread your sewing machine or sewing needle with matching thread. If you don't have matching thread, use thread a shade darker as it will blend in better. Put the zipper foot onto the sewing machine. Use a straight stitch on the machine or the backstitch if working by hand.

Step 5. Sew along the marked stitching lines as follows:

If stitching by machine:

➽ Move the needle so it's positioned on the right side of the presser foot. With the zipper closed, stitch across the bottom of the zipper starting at the seam. Turn at the corner of the marked stitch line and

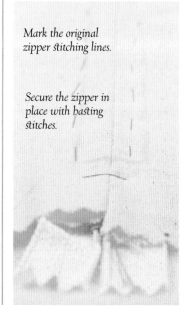

Mark the original zipper stitching lines.

Secure the zipper in place with basting stitches.

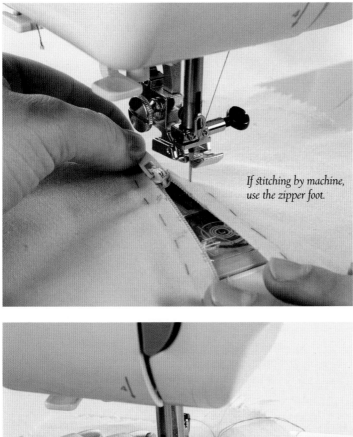

If stitching by machine, use the zipper foot.

Stitch to the end of the marked line and then stitch across the edge of the fabric.

continue half of the length of the stitching line.

➼ Move the needle to the down position, lift the presser foot, open the zipper, and lower the presser foot.

➼ Stitch to the end of the stitch line and stitch across the edge of the fabric. Fasten off before cutting the threads.

If stitching by hand:
Backstitch along the marked stitching lines, through the garment and the zipper tape, fasten off, and cut the threads.

Step 6. Line up the side of your zipper with the other folded edge of the garment, so the two fabric edges meet and cover the center of the zipper. Stitch as in step 5.

Step 7. If you ripped out stitches in the waistband or collar to release the zipper, res-titch them by hand using a slip stitch, catching the top of the zipper tape in the seam.

Separating Zippers

Separating zippers are replaced similarly to centered zippers (see page 156). The main difference is that you usually place the zipper tape between two pieces of fabric (the lining and the outer fabric) instead of just stitching it to the wrong side of the garment. Just make sure to pin the lining and the outer fabric securely so they line up after you have replaced the zipper; you might want to baste them together before you stitch them to ensure that they don't shift.

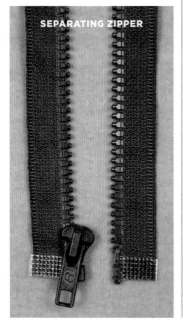

SEPARATING ZIPPER

Invisible Zippers

These wonderful zippers are usually found on dresses, but can sometimes be used in skirts and very fancy fitted tops, and even in a nice pillow. Pillows? Really? Yep. They actually fit very nicely along cording. It gives a pillow cover a really nice finished look while allowing it to be removed and washed if needed.

Step 1. Remove the broken zipper by very carefully picking out the stitches. If the stitches are very fine, use a dressmaker pin to pick them out and embroidery scissors to snip the threads. You will need to pick out the seam 2"

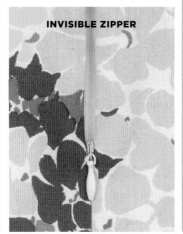

INVISIBLE ZIPPER

past where the zipper ends. If the zipper is sewn into a waistband or collar, unpick just enough to free it.

Step 2. Thread your sewing machine or sewing needle with an all-purpose thread. Color doesn't matter because the thread will be concealed. Secure a zipper foot onto the sewing machine. Use a straight stitch if you are working on the machine or a backstitch if working by hand.

Step 3. With the right side of the garment facing you, pin the right side of the open zipper to the garment so the edge of the zipper tape aligns with the cut edge of the seam allowance. Start stitching at the top and stitch down one side of the zipper tape as far as you can go. Align the zipper coil with the right side or guide of the zipper foot. Knot the threads or backstitch one or two stitches.

Step 4. Repeat step 3 to attach the other side.

Step 5. If you ripped out stitches along the top, restitch them by hand using a slip stitch, catching the top of the zipper tape in the seam.

Step 3: Pin right side of zipper to right side of fabric, lining up the edge of the tape with the cut edge of the seam allowance.

Step 4: Stitch from the top to the bottom aligning the zipper coil with the guide of the zipper foot.

INVISIBLE ZIPPER FOOT

For added precision, you can use an invisible zipper foot. Follow the instructions for installing an invisible zipper, being sure to align the open zipper coils in the guide on the bottom of the invisible zipper foot.

TOP VIEW

BOTTOM VIEW

zipper coils fit in groove

Fly Zippers

Fly zippers can be a bit tricky to replace, but well worth the effort to save your favorite jeans. Fly zippers are a variation of a lapped zipper (see box at right). The fabric flap is much wider, the zipper is a bit more industrial, and there is usually extra topstitching that is both decorative and utilitarian. Front fly zippers are only found in the center front of casual pants and skirts. I'm going to show you how to replace the fly on women's clothing, so for men's you will need to reverse the orientation of the instructions: stitching to the right of the teeth becomes stitching to the left.

Step 1. Before ripping out the zipper, mark the original zipper stitching lines with tailor's chalk and a ruler as a guide.

Step 2. Pick out all the stitches along the zipper to remove it from the fabric. If the zipper tape is stitched into the waistband, remove as few stitches as possible to release it from the seam. Avoid snagging or ripping out any of the decorative topstitching so you won't have to try to match the thread color later, which inevitably is impossible and always a pain. You should be able to release the zipper without ripping out the topstitching.

Step 3. With the closed zipper facing up, slip the left zipper tape into the waistband opening and pin or baste it to hold it in place. Align the teeth of the left side of the zipper with the finished edge that will be covered by the fabric. Use a basting stitch to hold the zipper in place.

Step 4. Put the zipper foot on your sewing machine. Sew with a straight stitch along the basting stitches as far as you can without the fly front fabric in the way. Open the fly.

Step 5. From the wrong side and using a backstitch, finish sewing the zipper tape to the fabric by hand.

Step 6. Close the fly all the way and position the front flap over the right side of the zipper. Slip the remaining top of the zipper tape into the waistband and stitch it in place with a basting stitch or pin it so it stays in place. Line up the zipper tape with the stitch line

basting

stitching

you marked in step 1. Pin or baste the zipper in place.

Step 7. Working from the inside, backstitch the zipper tape in place by hand, following the basting stitches as your guide. Catch all the layers of fabric, but just a few threads from the outer layer so no stitches show through to the front. For extra support, work a bar of backstitches at the base of the zipper. Restitch the waistband seam, catching the top of the zipper tapes in the seam.

BASIC LAPPED ZIPPERS

The dressed-down version of a fly, a basic lapped zipper is most commonly used in skirts. Just like with the fly in your favorite jeans, the zipper is concealed, but topstitching is visible along just one side.

◆▸ To replace a basic lapped zipper, follow steps 1 through 6 from the Fly Zippers instructions.

◆▸ Finish by using a straight stitch on the sewing machine (a backstitch if you are working by hand); starting at the bottom of the zipper, sew across the bottom, then up the outside edge of the zipper along the marked line.

◆▸ Remove all the basting stitches and marks. If you removed the zipper from the waistband, now is a good time to stitch the waist back in place.

completing

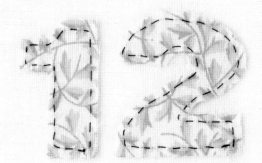

Getting Fancy

I don't have a lot of fancy clothing, but I want to keep the items I *do* have in top-notch shape for years to come. Items made of lace, leather, suede, pile fabrics such as velvet, and specialty knit fabrics all need a little extra care when it comes to mending (and washing, for that matter, but more on that in chapter 14). In this chapter I'll show you ways you can keep your favorite special pieces in the best possible condition, even that threadbare Little League T-shirt.

Lacework

ace is especially dear to me, not because of its frill, but because I made most of the lace items I own from lace handmade by my Grandma Phyllis and my Great-grandma Elda. I want to keep it in great condition. Lace can be difficult to mend because of the tangle of beautiful stitch work. I learned a lesson from a 1910 women's magazine on how to keep all my lace in good repair. The magazine referenced Italian lace markets and the mending businesses that accompanied them and provided a very helpful series of tips for lace mending.

Repairing a Hole

Step 1. First, try to find a piece of lace that is similar to what you are mending. If you cannot find anything similar, use a little piece of tulle instead.

Step 2. If you are using tulle, place an undamaged area of

> **REPAIR TIP**
> If you are repairing a large area, it's best to use a similar lace and not tulle. Once you stitch it all together, a lace with slightly different lace design or patterning will be less noticeable than a big gaping hole, filled only with tulle.

the lace over the tulle and iron it so the lace impresses the tulle behind it. Pin the impressed tulle or substitute lace piece (from step 1), with the right side up, to the wrong side of the garment, behind the hole.

Step 3. Use a fine nylon thread (or, as suggested by Italian lace menders of the nineteenth century, a hair from your own head) and stitch all the loose threads to the tulle. This will secure the lace/tulle

REPAIRING A HOLE

patch to the fabric and hopefully prevent any further opening of the hole. Trim away any excess threads.

Repairing a Tear

If the lace you love is torn, you can easily and quickly stitch it back together.

Step 1. Select a fine nylon or silk thread that is a similar color to the lace you are repairing. Thread your sewing needle using a single strand and knot one end.

Step 2. Secure the thread in the lace by working a small stitch and then stitching back through the center of the knot.

Step 3. Sew a round of small stitches all around the perimeter of the tear to secure the loose threads.

Step 4. Use a ladder stitch (see page 52) to close the tear. Fasten off the thread.

REPAIRING A TEAR

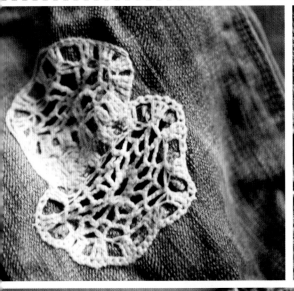

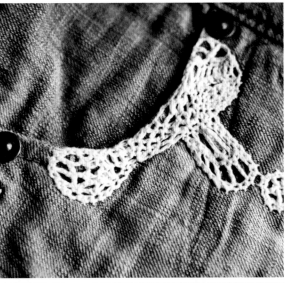

The holes in these jeans were original to the new pair Maja Blomqvist bought. But when she got them home, she wasn't so thrilled by the look. Inspired by crocheted tablecloths, Maya applied crochet motifs to cover, close, and decorate the holes, transforming the jeans into a one-of-a-kind favorite.

Leather and Suede

*Y*our favorite leather jacket, so sexy and cool, that is, until it wears thin and rips. Not so cool anymore, is it? Well, it is a little trickier to fix leather and suede, but it's definitely possible. Sometimes you can get by with a patch and glue. However, if you need to do some stitching, use heavyweight thread that is a shade darker than the material you are repairing and you'll definitely need a thimble to protect your fingers. If you are repairing really thick leather, grab a pair of needle-nose pliers to help you pull the needle through.

Leather Repair Tool Box

Because of leather's animal nature, you need a special set of tools to make the best repairs possible. Sharp stiff needles, thimbles to keep your fingers from bleeding, sharp little pointy scissors for detail-oriented trimming, strong thread, and for really thick leathers, pliers to pull the needle through. A lot of these items will already be in your mending tool kit, but if you are doing a lot of leather-related repair, it might be a good idea to have a little kit just for leather and suede repair. Here's what you need to stock it:

Patches. Keep small scraps of leather and suede, in shades of brown and black. For a more decorative look, you can use any sturdy fabric; upholstery fabrics, oilcloth, vinyl, corduroy, and denims all work nicely.

Glues. For a small tear, "liquid stitch" leather glue will hold it together, especially if it is backed with a small piece of muslin fabric. Most leather glues are clear and very similar to rubberized superglue. In a pinch, you can use a superglue to repair an unsightly tear.

Needles. Leather working needles have a sharp, triangular point, designed specifically to pierce leather, vinyl, and other thick plastic fabrics. For thinner leathers, you can use regular sharps, but leather needles will glide more smoothly through your work.

Snips. You will need to trim away and clean up damaged

WHAT IS SUEDE ANYWAY?

What is suede, and how is it different from full-grain leather? Suede is a type of leather that is made from the underside of an animal hide. The benefits of suede are that it is soft, pliable, and it looks really nice. But it has a downside. Being made from the underside of a hide, suede is really porous. It is pretty susceptible to staining because it so readily absorbs everything. Even dirt and oil from your hands can stain suede, so you should keep your hands nice and clean and dry while mending. If you have a stain to clean up or want to prevent them in the first place, check out page 200 for caring for and preventing damage to your leather and suede items.

areas with sharp, fine-pointed scissors. Having a really sharp pair on hand will save you much time and frustration.

Thread. When mending anything made of leather, a general rule to follow when choosing a thread is to match the weight of the material used to make the garment. Usually, lightweight leathers are sewn with all-purpose sewing thread or top-stitching thread, often referred to as "utility" thread. Medium to heavyweight leathers and suedes are sewn with waxed nylon, cotton, or linen threads. Waxed threads glide through leather better; if you can't find waxed thread, you can slide a heavy cotton thread through beeswax to make it more suitable for sewing leather.

Pliers. If you have a particularly thick piece of leather, it's helpful to use needle-nose or flat-nose pliers to hold the needle while sewing.

Thimble. The first time I sewed leather I forgot this important tool and shortly into the project, my index finger started to bleed from pushing the needle into the material.

Leather repair kits. If you are trying to match a specific color, a leather repair kit might just be the way to go. They usually cost about $20 and are available at shoe stores, department stores, online, and even some grocery stores. Good kits contain a subpatch and everything you need, including detailed instructions, to create a patch close to the color of the leather you need to repair. There are two types, air activated and heat activated. Heat-activated kits work okay on things like jackets, but tend to be less successful on shoes, small gloves, and upholstery.

Patching a Hole in Leather and Suede

Step 1. Trim the hole into a nice smooth oval shape. Make sure to trim past the damaged material.

Step 2. Cut a patch from a scrap of leather or suede as close as possible to the color of the item (or purchase a leather patch), so that it overlaps the hole by ¼" on all sides.

Step 3. Apply a small bead of glue to the wrong side of the

leather being repaired (where it will overlap) and all around the edges of the patch, then press the two pieces together (right side of patch to wrong side of garment). Hold the patch in place until it stays by itself. Follow the instructions on your glue for the recommended cure time.

PATCHING A HOLE

FOR EXTRA SUPPORT

If you are applying a leather patch over an area that receives a lot of stress (like elbows), it's a good idea to apply some reinforcement by stitching the patch to the garment after the glue has dried. Secure the thread to the underside of the material. Use an overcast stitch (see page 48) to tack the edge of the patch to the material. Fasten off.

Mending a Tear in Leather

It's a sad day when you brush past something, get snagged, instinctively jerk away, and — *rippppp!* — you are left with a jagged tear. Thankfully, you can stitch it back up so all that is visible are little dots of thread from the front.

Step 1. Thread your needle with an 18" length of utility thread.

Step 2. Secure the thread to the material so the knot is on the underside of the fabric and make a small stitch near the base of the tear.

Step 3. Holding the torn edges together, make a small stitch directly across the tear from the first stitch. Just take up a minimal amount of material; you want as small of a stitch as possible. You're working on the right side of the fabric, pulling the thread taut between stitches to close the tear.

Step 4. Make a small stitch directly above the previous stitch.

Step 5. Repeat steps 3 and 4 until you've worked up the entire length of the tear. Fasten off the thread.

Step 6. Grab your glue and dab it on the underside of the tear to give it a little bit more strength and staying power.

REMINDS ME OF STITCHES

Have you ever cut yourself and needed stitches? Well, when you repair leather, you want it to look like a scar from getting stitches. Think of a little line with little dots along each side. When I cut my finger with a rotary cutter a few springs ago, I needed five stitches to make my finger right again. I have to say, I was pretty disappointed with their stitching smarts. Maybe next time I'll stitch it up myself. It's just a series of knots after all.

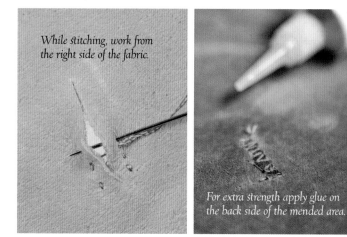

While stitching, work from the right side of the fabric.

For extra strength apply glue on the back side of the mended area.

Pile Fabrics

Velvet, chenille, shag, and polar fleece are all great examples of pile fabrics; they're plush, thick, and often luxurious fabrics. Because of the way pile fabrics are made, they have a whole different set of mending and fixing problems that need to be addressed. Creases, holes, and tears all need to be handled a little differently. To keep your favorite Renaissance-style velvet cape in tip-top shape, flip over to page 170 to read about some general care and damage prevention ideas.

HOW ARE PILE FABRICS MADE?

When I took my first weaving class, we wove pile fabric as part of our first sampler. We ran the warp threads vertically and wove the weft threads in and through the warps. To create a pile fabric, we wove a supplemental weft thread that was pulled up into loops. We used a pencil to make the loops, and then we simply cut them. Pile fabrics have pretty much been woven that way since multiharness looms came into being. Handmade pile rugs are made in a similar way, by tying a string around warp threads, knotting them, and snipping the ends to a unified height.

Removing Creases

When a pile fabric, such as velvet, is stored for a long time or worn quite a bit, deep creases often form. Once pile fabrics are creased, they really like to stay that way. Unlike a cotton or linen cloth, you can't just drop it on your ironing board and give it a good pressing. To unkink the pile fibers and remove the creases, you need to apply steam. As a last resort, you can try to iron them out.

Gently steam. Hang the garment in your bathroom while you are taking a hot shower. Hopefully this room-sized steam bath will have the desired effect. If not, try the directed steaming method.

Directed steam. Grab your handheld steamer and steam the fabric in large sweeping strokes on the lowest setting. Slowly turn up the steam level until the creases release. If you get to the maximum setting and the creases are still there, you will need to bring out the iron. If you don't have a handheld steamer, you can use your flat iron. Crank it up to the highest steam setting and sweep the iron over the fabric with the point facing down. Just be careful not to touch the fabric.

Pressing Pile Fabric

Pressing pile fabric does take a specialized tool, but don't despair, you can make your

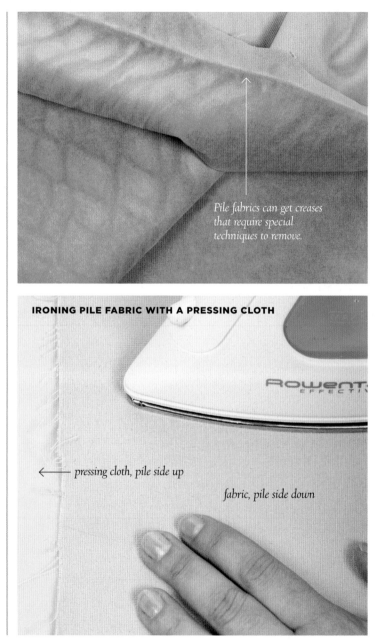

Pile fabrics can get creases that require special techniques to remove.

IRONING PILE FABRIC WITH A PRESSING CLOTH

←——— *pressing cloth, pile side up*

fabric, pile side down

own with a little ingenuity. A pressing cloth is an easy tool to find at home, because a dig around your stash will probably reveal what you need; a terrycloth towel is a good choice, or any fabric with a bit of pile itself. If you can't find a suitable fabric, a trip to the local fabric store and a few dollars should do the trick.

What is a pressing cloth and what does it do? Well, it's a cloth that protects the fabric you love from the horrors of a hot iron. In the case of pile fabrics, it helps to keep the piles standing up straight. By placing the pressing cloth

DIY PRESSING CLOTH

Select a fabric that has a similar if not longer length pile than the one you want to press. Cut a piece that is large enough to cover the ironing board. Finish the edges with a zigzag stitch, overlock stitch, or a blanket stitch if working by hand.

and the pile fabric right sides together, the pile is pushed into the pile of the pressing cloth, so it stays straight instead of being smashed.

Another great "pressing cloth" for pile fabrics — a needle board — isn't a cloth at all. It's a thin board covered in many short needles and is by far the best tool for resetting pile fabric. Needle boards can be pricey and hard to find, but if you have a lot of velvets, it's worth the search. Antique stores are a great place to look, as well as auction websites like eBay.

While all these pressing techniques are geared toward pile fabric care, they can be applied to all of your clothing in general. Pressing is pretty key in helping to keep your whole wardrobe looking smart. Make a tailor's ham from muslin and use it with a pressing cloth for all your other pressing needs, too.

Using a Pressing Cloth

Step 1. Place the pressing cloth or needle board right side up on the ironing board.

Step 2. Place the cloth pile side down on the pressing cloth.

Step 3. Set the heat to the appropriate setting (silk for silk, polyester for polyester) and gently press (don't glide) the iron over the back of the fabric. Press the iron onto the fabric and lift up; repeat pressing and lifting the iron over the whole area. If you do glide the iron across the fabric while applying pressure, always move it in the same direction, left to right for instance. Increase the pressure until the crease is gone completely.

Using a Tailor's Ham

When you are ironing something that isn't nice and flat, like that big velvet Renaissance cape I mentioned earlier, you will need to use a different tool. This one has a pretty funny name: it's a velvet tailor's ham. Seriously, it is really called a tailor's ham and the reason is simply that it looks like a tasty holiday ham, only without the cloves sticking out of it. A tailor's ham is a very useful tool for pressing all types of fabrics, not just pile fabrics, especially when you are trying to press shape into a flat seam.

To make: Check out page 174 to learn how to make your own. If you will be ironing a lot of pile fabrics, make the ham out of a pile fabric instead of muslin.

To use: Turn the garment inside out. In the case of a sleeve, place the ham on the inside of the sleeve and press as shown below.

Repairing Holes and Tears

When a pile fabric is torn, what unfortunately happens is all those little cut ends start to fall out. You can darn or sew or patch a tear, but you will never be able to replace those missing threads. Of course, prevention is key. If you start to see an area of the fabric wearing out, apply one of the preventative reinforcing patches I talk about in chapter 4 (see page 61). If it wears out completely and you need to do more than just reinforce, here is how you set things right again.

Stitch it. Work a blanket stitch (see page 52) around the perimeter of the tear. Catch all the loose threads so they will not unravel further. Use an interior patching method (see page 62) to close the hole.

Glue it. Dab a little fray-preventative glue on the underside of the tear. You want to make sure that you do not get any glue on the front side of the fabric or it will mat the pile.

Patch it. If the tear is large enough you will need to apply a patch. Working from the inside of the garment, follow instructions on page 62 to patch the hole from the inside.

Fluff it up. Take a fine-toothed comb and run it through the pile so it covers up the stitching. Or use a needle board to press it and reset the pile.

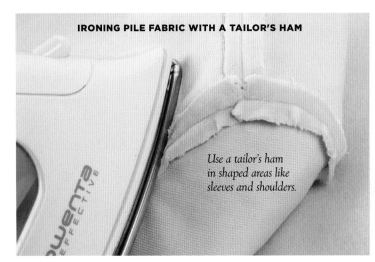

IRONING PILE FABRIC WITH A TAILOR'S HAM

Use a tailor's ham in shaped areas like sleeves and shoulders.

STITCHING A TEAR

Fluffing the pile will conceal the stitching.

Stretch Fabrics

~·~

*S*tretch fabrics make up some of our most heavily used wardrobe items: T-shirts, gym clothes, and underwear. Stretch fabrics can be tricky to fix because you're using threads that don't stretch to repair a stretchy surface. When you insert something inflexible into something flexible, it is going to cause the flexible item to contort and not function as it did in its natural state. In the case of overstretched collars and button bands, like Francesca's sweater project on page 144, this can be great. But if you are trying to patch a hole in your favorite T-shirt where your belt snagged it, the usual stitching method isn't so helpful. By using these few tricks and tips you can get stretch fabrics back in working condition in no time.

Repairing a Tear

Step 1. Cut a piece of light fusible knit interfacing that is slightly longer and wider than the tear.

Step 2. Abut the edges of the tear and apply the fusible webbing to the wrong side of the fabric, behind the tear.

Step 3. Using a machine, zigzag stitch over the tear to stabilize it and reinforce the fusible webbing. By hand, work a running stitch around the tear and then a ladder stitch to reinforce the area around the tear.

REPAIRING A TEAR

back

front

Patching a Hole

While you can use any fabric you choose to repair a hole in your knit fabric, I highly recommend selecting a similar fabric for the patch.

Follow the directions on page 62 to apply a patch to the inside, or see page 66 for a decorative exterior patch. Instead of straight stitching though, use the zigzag stitch. It has more flexibility than a straight stitch so the fabric will not bunch or gather.

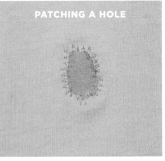

PATCHING A HOLE

Reinforcing Seams

On stretch fabrics, it's pretty common for seams to stretch out. Usually the shoulder seams are the worst. You can zigzag stitch a length of twill tape along the seam of a shoulder to stabilize the fabric.

MAKE YOUR OWN TAILOR'S HAM

by Kristin Roach

This great pressing tool is so easy to make and it's so helpful. It will take a few tries to get the hang of how to use it, but over time it will really improve your pressing results.

What You'll Need

Template for ham (below)

Muslin, velvet, and upholstery fabric scraps slightly larger than the template

Batting, enough for 2 pieces the size of the template

Shredded paper to use as filling

Mending supply kit (see page 24)

Sewing machine (optional)

What You'll Do

Step 1. Use the template to cut one piece of muslin, one piece of upholstery fabric, and two pieces of batting.

Step 2. Layer the fabrics and batting in the following order:

� batting

� upholstery or velvet and muslin fabric, right sides together

� batting

Step 3. Stitch around the edge of the layered fabrics, using a ½" seam allowance and leaving a 3" gap. Turn the layers right side out through the opening.

Step 4. Stuff the ham as tightly as you can with the shredded paper. Use a ladder stitch to close the gap. Fasten off and trim the threads.

TEMPLATE

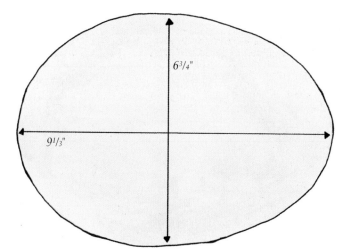

$6^3/_4$"

$9^1/_3$"

SWEDISH FISH WALLET

by Kristin Roach

When your favorite wallet is stained, scuffed, torn, and not looking so fancy, you can fix it up quite easily. You can even update its look with a scrap of oilcloth and a cute design. Say you have an unsightly spot on your wallet that's driving you nuts, like a pen mark, ink, or a tear. Instead of just patching it, you cut out the whole area in a cute design and refresh the look of the wallet. In my case, I was inspired by the Swedish Fish gummy candy for the cutout design; someone else might like a little cat head cutout or a flower. Just use your imagination!

What You'll Need

1 leather or faux leather wallet or purse

2" x 3" piece of oilcloth or leather

Fish template

Utility knife

1 hand-sewing leather needle

Topstitching thread

Thimble

What You'll Do

Step 1. Draw the shape you want for the cutout on paper, or copy the fish template at right and cut it out.

Step 2. Trace this shape onto the area of the wallet where you would like the reverse appliqué patch to go.

Step 3. Use a utility knife to carefully cut away the material along the traced lines. Work slowly and do not try to cut through the leather with one cut. Instead, score the line you marked onto the wallet, and then slowly cut it deeper until you are all the way through. Use a new sharp blade.

Step 4. Cut a piece of oilcloth that is ⅛" to ¼" larger than the design cutout.

Step 5. Push the oilcloth patch through the hole you cut and smooth it out behind the hole. For small designs, use the tip of your needle to adjust the position of the patch.

Step 6. Use a double strand of thread, knotted at one end, to sew the patch into the cut-out. Secure the thread to the underside of the fabric, and then work a blanket stitch (see page 52) all around the edge of the cutout design, catching the patch with the tip of your needle as you work each stitch. When you get all the way to the end, fasten off the thread.

TEMPLATE

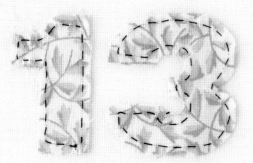

Decorative Accents

Accents add a special touch to any item in your wardrobe. A little bit of beadwork, embroidery, or decorative gems can really class up any plain design. Unfortunately, decorative accents of any kind are susceptible to snagging and coming loose. This is too bad, because with strings sticking out and beads missing, a classy piece can look pretty dumpy. All is not lost, though. There are easy ways to fix any kind of accent.

Beads and Sequins

*U*sually, but not always, *beads and sequins are attached to fabric in pretty much the same way. A bead is slipped onto the sewing needle, a stitch is worked by inserting the needle back through the fabric next to the bead, and then the next bead or sequin is slipped on. Sometimes a cap seed bead is added so the thread goes just through the hole in the bead and not around the side.*

When one bead falls off or the thread that connects them all snaps, the decorative work will start to unravel one bead at a time. Just like every other mending project, I highly recommend fixing beadwork as soon as you notice it starting to come undone.

Unraveling Threads

When the thread breaks that holds all those great beads on your favorite bag or sweater, keep them from continuing to slip way by fixing and securing the thread.

Step 1. Select a thread that is similar to the original. Thread a single strand through a beading needle and knot one end.

Step 2. Secure the thread to the back of the fabric by working one stitch.

Step 3. Run the needle through the last five beads that are still strung and are closest to the area with missing beads.

Step 4. Bring the needle to the right side. Slide one or two missing beads on the needle and run the thread through them and to the wrong side of the fabric.

Step 5. Repeat step 4 to restitch any beads that are loose or have fallen off.

Step 6. Once all the loose beads are reattached, run the needle and new thread through the next few beads on the opposite side of the broken thread.

Step 7. Bring the thread to the wrong side and work several backstitches over the loose thread to secure it to the back of the fabric.

UNRAVELING THREADS

Step 3: Run thread through the last five beads that are still strung.

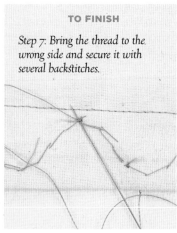

TO FINISH

Step 7: Bring the thread to the wrong side and secure it with several backstitches.

Adding Beads and Sequins

You may want to add beads to your clothing to cover or embellish areas that have been mended. They are pretty quick and easy to apply and can draw the eye away from a flaw.

Attaching Rows of Beads

Step 1. Mark out the path for your beads with a fabric marking pen before you start stitching.

Step 2. Secure the thread with a knot on the wrong side of the fabric at the beginning of the stitch line.

Step 3. Bring the thread to the front of the work at the beginning of the stitch line.

Step 4. Slide several beads, about a 1" worth, onto the needle and hold it up against the fabric.

Step 5. Make a stitch into the fabric so the beads lie flat against the fabric.

Step 6. Bring the needle to the right side again and repeat steps 4 and 5 until you have added as many beads as you want. Fasten off your thread.

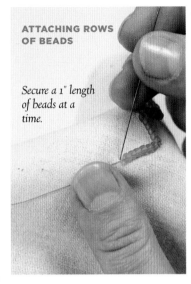

ATTACHING ROWS OF BEADS

Secure a 1" length of beads at a time.

Attaching Scattered Beads

Step 1. Mark out the path for your beads with a fabric marking pen before you start stitching.

Step 2. Secure the thread with a knot on the wrong side of the fabric at the beginning of the stitch line.

Step 3. Bring the thread to the right side of the fabric where you want the first bead to go; slip a bead on the needle and slide it up against the fabric.

Step 4. Insert the needle into the fabric right next to the edge of the bead.

Step 5. Repeat steps 3 and 4 until you have added all the beads you would like. Fasten off and trim the thread.

Stitching on Sequins

Step 1. Mark out the path for your sequins with a fabric marking pen before you start stitching.

Step 2. Secure the thread with a knot on the wrong side of the fabric at the beginning of the stitch line.

Step 3. Bring the thread up through the fabric and through the center of the first sequin and then around the edge of

the sequin back to the wrong side of the fabric.

Step 4. Stitch up through the hole and around the edge of the sequin at least one more time.

Step 5. Carry the thread along on the wrong side. Sew on another sequin or fasten off and trim the loose threads.

QUICK FIX

If you are out and about and notice your sequins starting to fall off one by one, keep them from unraveling further by covering the area with a piece of packaging tape. If you are in a setting where you need a little more professionalism than packaging tape allows, tie the two broken thread ends together and put any loose beads and sequins in a zip-top food storage bag. No food storage bag? Well, grab that packaging tape again and put all the beads on a strip of it, then fold the tape onto itself. While you may have to work a little bit to get them off the tape, it is still better than losing them.

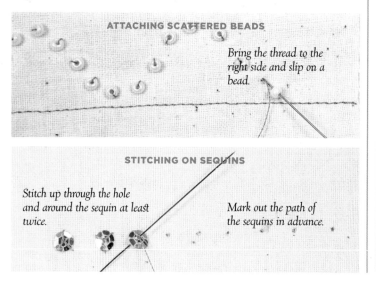

ATTACHING SCATTERED BEADS

Bring the thread to the right side and slip on a bead.

STITCHING ON SEQUINS

Stitch up through the hole and around the sequin at least twice.

Mark out the path of the sequins in advance.

Caitlin Stevens Andrews scored a thrift store find with this cashmere sweater — only to discover it had a few holes in it. She transformed the holes into a beautiful feature by applying embroidery and beadwork. Using the buttonhole stitch and embroidery thread, she first stitched around the hole to stabilize it, and then embellished it with seed and bugle beads. She chose a flower motif, but suggests exploring bubbles, eyes, planets, and fruit for more cosmic designs.

Sequins or Beads with a Seed Bead Cap

Step 1. Mark out the path for your sequins with a fabric marking pen before you start stitching.

Step 2. Secure the thread with a knot on the wrong side of the fabric at the beginning of the stitch line.

Step 3. Bring the thread up through the fabric to the front and slide a sequin or a larger bead and a seed bead on the needle.

Step 4. Stitch over the side of the seed bead, back through the center of the sequin, and to the wrong side of the fabric. Fasten off the thread or stitch on more sequins.

Step 5. Repeat steps 3 and 4 to stitch on more sequins or fasten off and trim the loose threads.

Prestrung Sequins

Step 1. Mark out the path for your sequins with a fabric marking pen before you start stitching.

Step 2. Lay out the string of sequins on the marked line.

Step 3. Secure the thread on the back of the fabric and bring it to the right side at the beginning of the stitch line.

Step 4. Work a straight stitch between the sequins and around the thread of the sequin strand every few sequins.

Step 5. Keep working stitches for the length of the strand, and then bring the thread to the wrong side and fasten off.

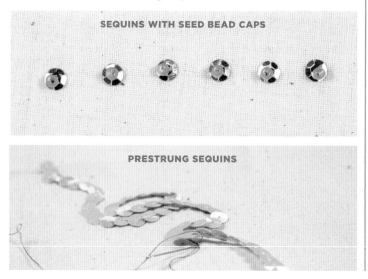

SEQUINS WITH SEED BEAD CAPS

PRESTRUNG SEQUINS

Decorative Stones

Decorative gemstones come in a variety of shapes and sizes, but there are only a few types commonly used in sewing and mending. There are stones with holes, which you apply just like beads, or flat-backed stones that can be attached with glue, and some can even be heat activated. Simple flat-backed stones are the easiest to use as replacements on clothing.

Replacing Flat-Backed Stones

Apply a bit of glue to the back of the stone and hold it in place until it is set. Avoid moving or disturbing it for several minutes. I like using non-water-soluble glue such as an epoxy.

Fixing Rhinestones

Rhinestones are probably one of the most popular decorative stones to add to clothing. They are applied with a dab of glue if they are flat or they are secured with a clamp setting if they have prongs. Sometimes all you have to do is tighten the prongs if the rhinestones are loose.

WHY DO RHINESTONES TURN YELLOW?

Rhinestones are made by adhering foil onto the back side of a piece of glass (or plastic in contemporary manufacturing) with a bit of glue. Rhinestones from the '30s, '40s, and '50s were made with glue that, over time, degraded and turned yellow. If you have a garment with yellowed rhinestones, cleaning the stones well will help, but they will never be crystal clear. The only way to fix them is to replace the glue and foil on the back or to replace the whole stone. Replacing the foil may be worth it if the stone is a unique shape.

When Maja Blomqvist found her coat lining cracking, she created these heart-shaped folkloric patches made from scrap cloth secured with Vliesofix adhesive paper. She finished off the edges with blanket and cross-stitch done with yarn.

Decorative Stitching

*U*se decorative stitching to cover up stains, accent patching, and bring a little beauty to mended areas. Before you start stitching, press fusible interfacing to the back of the garment where you plan to stitch.

Hand Embroidery

I love stitching embroidery by hand. You can meander and trace and use loads of colors. Each mended area becomes its own work of art. To get a handle on the art of embroidery:

➻ Sketch it out before you start stitching it on the fabric.

➻ While embroidery floss is always a good choice, try using two-ply wools to change things up a little bit (crewel embroidery work).

➻ Use a hoop to stabilize the fabric while working.

Here are some basic embroidery stitches to get you started. If you get inspired and want to try more stitches, see Resources for more books on the topic.

French knot: Bring the needle to the front of the work at the desired location for the French knot. Put tension on the thread with your left thumb. Twist the thread around the needle twice and insert the needle back into the fabric right next to where it came out of the fabric. Keep tension on the thread and cinch the knot down right next to the fabric.

Backstitch: Bring the needle to the front by drawing it through the fabric. Move a stitch length backward and insert the needle back into the fabric, and then draw the needle through the fabric two stitch lengths ahead. Repeat.

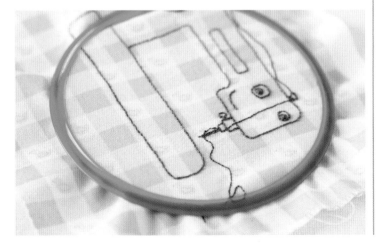

FRENCH KNOT

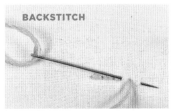

BACKSTITCH

Satin stitch: Satin stitches are made by working long, straight stitches closely together to fill a shape. If you are following an outlined shape, make sure the stitches you are working are covering up the marked lines so they do not show through.

Machine Embroidery

By placing a stabilizing fabric like interfacing on the back of the area to be mended, you can use an embroidery machine or a regular sewing machine with decorative stitch setting to stitch over tears, holes, and stains. If your machine isn't capable of embroidery, even simple stitches like the zigzag stitch can look fun and decorative when worked in bright colors along a hemline.

There are two types of machine embroidery:

❧ Free motion machine embroidery is basically you and your sewing machine with the feed dogs lowered, moving the fabric around to stitch an area over and over again to build up a design.

❧ Digital embroidery machines are machines that are either an embroidery-only machine or a sewing machine that has a removable embroidery unit. Embroidery machines don't work the same way sewing machines do. They don't have feed dogs that move the fabric; instead, the fabric stays in the same place while the needle moves to stitch the design.

If you are considering buying an embroidery machine there are three things to consider:

❧ Whether it can be used as a sewing machine

❧ The size of the hoop(s), which determines the maximum embroidery area

❧ Software and design options, and inclusions

PRACTICE MAKES PERFECT

Try repairing and embroidering a practice tear on a scrap piece of fabric before attempting it on an original garment.

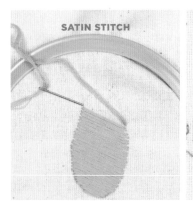

SATIN STITCH

BASIC SEWING MACHINE EMBROIDERY

Here are some things to consider about machine embroidery:

Hooping: Embroidery machines come with a hoop that holds and stretches the fabric during embroidery.

Stabilizers: The area of fabric being embroidered needs extra support for the stitches. Support is given by stretching the fabric in a hoop, and by backing the fabric area with a stabilizer, usually a stiff interfacing-type fabric.

COVER IT WITH TRIM

If your trim is starting to unravel, use a blanket or zigzag stitch to keep the unraveling edge from unraveling further. Stitch the loose trim piece back in place with the prick stitch (see page 50). The strategic placement of decorative trim can help heal all kinds of clothing wounds.

●→ Ribbons, hem tape, and rickrack cover up mended areas.

●→ Bias tape covers up torn edges (see Binding Basics *on page* 149).

●→ Lacy motifs and trims can be stitched or fused onto areas that need a little cover-up.

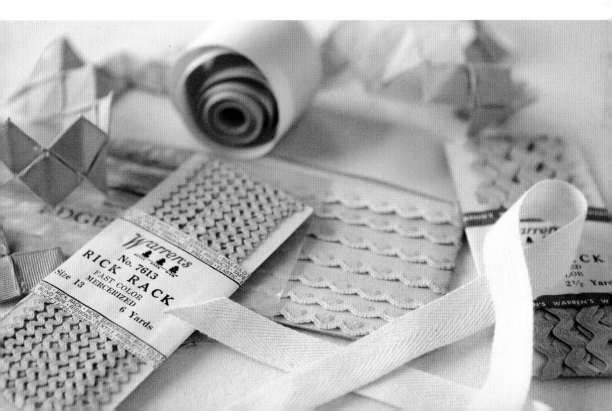

RICKRACK SKIRT UPDO

by Kristin Roach

I was really happy when I found this particular gray corduroy skirt, but when I wore it around for the first time, I soon discovered that it had this strange spattering of spots along the bottom. No worries; by digging around in my sewing stash I found the perfect thing to not only cover up those grease stains, but to make the skirt much cuter in the process. Rickrack! Instead of trying to make a straight line with it, I opted to play a bit of connect the dots. While I used rickrack for this skirt, you can apply any flat decorative trim using the sewing method described below. Just think how fun and glitzy some beading or pretty ribbon would look. Take a look at the fabric and see what you already have in your stash that would really make the skirt shine.

Step 1. If you are trying to cover up something like a smattering of grease or a bendy organic line of ink, use a fabric marking pen to draw your stitching line, covering the offending stains. Don't be confined to just one line; you can draw two or more lines to make it really fun and interesting.

Step 2. Working from the side seam, pin your rickrack in place. I like to lay it all out first, then adjust a bit for aesthetic and cover-up reasons.

Step 3. Because the lines are so curvy, you might want to use hand stitching to attach the rickrack. A simple running stitch will do the job well. For this project, I used my machine.

Step 4. Apply a little bit of fray prevention glue to the beginning and end of each piece of rickrack so it won't unravel over time, or turn under the ends before stitching it to the garment.

THRIFT STORE TREASURE

Going to the thrift store is always an adventure. You never know what you will find, what item will grab you, or what will inspire you to act. There are so many bland skirts and shirts just begging to be updated, fixed, and made unique. The fun for me is picking up items with a classic shape and then having fun making them my own with a few simple alterations. Instead of seeing damage as something to avoid, it's a starting point for creative mending techniques.

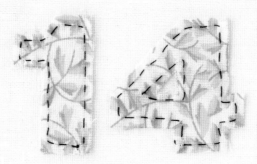

Care and Prevention

Taking care of your clothing while it's in great condition is one of the best ways to prevent them from having to be mended in the first place. Here are some of the best tips for deciphering care instructions, washing and drying; storing your clothing in the off-season, and removing stains before they set.

Washing and Drying

*W*hen you look at the care label inside your clothing, it will reveal a lot of great advice on how to wash, dry, and press the item. By following the care guidelines, your clothing will last much longer than if you just toss everything in the washer and dryer on high heat. After all, the lint in your dryer is your clothing coming apart, one little fuzz at a time. Here are some tips for cleaning our clothes in ways that will extend their life.

Washing Tips

Believe it or not, extra detergent can damage clothing, so use the recommended amount. The general order of operation for top-loading washers is: start the water, add the detergent, and then add the clothing. For front-loading machines, the clothes go in the front of the machine and the detergent goes in a special location and the water filters in once the cycle begins. Here are some other tips:

➻ zip up zippers

➻ empty pockets

➻ turn brightly colored clothing inside out

➻ sort clothing by weight, color, and how soiled they are

➻ to save energy, presoak clothing and wash and rinse in cold water

➻ only use the hot wash setting for extremely soiled clothing and whites

➻ cold wash and rinse is best for wools

Machine-Drying Tips

Do you know that your delicate clothes will overheat if you dry them with heavy clothes? So dry delicates separately and remove them from the machine before they are completely dry and lay them flat or hang them to finish drying.

While you may not think of silk as an animal fiber, it is. And, just like wool, it will mat, felt, and distort in the dryer. Most wool and silk clothing benefits from dry cleaning or hand washing. In general, if care instructions are not specified, if the garment is handmade, or if the tag has long since gone missing, the safest bet is to lay animal fibers flat to dry.

Lint may not seem like a big danger, but leaving excess lint in the dryer creates a serious fire hazard. Clean out the lint trap after every load to keep things safe as well as energy efficient. Once or twice a year remove the lint trap completely and soak it in hot soapy water to remove fabric softener buildup. Over time, it will clog all those fine mesh holes.

Clothesline Drying Tips

When I moved recently, I was oddly excited about the tattered clothesline hanging out in the backyard. I had always wanted one, and it was the first thing I repaired. By using a clothesline you can save money, your clothes, and your dryer. You know all that lint that's collected in the lint trap each load? Yeah, well, that's your clothing! With each load, you are wearing them down. Line drying prevents that.

Of course you'll want to use your dryer at times, especially in the winter. But by using your dryer less, you prolong its life. More savings! Or at least, fewer big purchases. I would be happy to keep my dryer working for the next 15 years or so.

To avoid weird drapes: Dry shirts and socks upside down. Dry pants, jeans, shorts, skirts, and undies from their waistbands.

To hang big things: Drape towels, blankets, and sheets over two strings of clotheslines.

To save clothespins: Hang clothes that are next to each other with one pin by overlapping each item slightly.

To have less wrinkles: Give your clothes a good shake and snap before hanging them up.

To avoid damage to delicate items: Hang lacy, silky, fancy pants, shirts, and such on hangers and pin the hangers to the line.

To avoid sun bleaching: Hang your brights inside out to preserve their fun colors.

To let the sun do its awesome natural bleaching: Hang whites right side out.

To save time: If you hang all your clothes up in your closet, hang them on hangers on the clothesline *or* take them down and put them on hangers right away. Coming off the line they are easy and quick to hang versus being wrinkled and tangled up in a basket.

To keep it clean: Wipe down your clothesline at least once a month. I've actually added it to my weekly routine. It's outside and gets dirty, and that dirt will transfer to your clothes if you don't clean it.

CARE PICTOGRAPHS

Here is a key to numerous standard symbols that represent the types
of cleaning and care you should give your clothing.

WASHING

- Machine Wash, Cold
- Machine Wash, Cold, Permanent Press
- Machine Wash, Cold, Gentle Cycle
- Machine Wash, Warm
- Machine Wash, Warm, Permanent Press
- Machine Wash, Warm, Gentle Cycle
- Machine Wash, Hot
- Machine Wash, Hot, Permanent Press
- Machine Wash, Hot, Gentle Cycle
- Hand Wash
- Do Not Wash

BLEACHING

- Bleach as Needed
- Non-chlorine Bleach
- Do Not Bleach

IRONING

- Iron, Steam or Dry, with Low Heat
- Iron, Steam or Dry, with Medium Heat
- Iron, Steam or Dry, with High Heat
- Do Not Iron with Steam
- Do Not Iron

DRYING

- Tumble Dry, No Heat
- Tumble Dry, No Heat, Permanent Press
- Tumble Dry, No Heat, Gentle Cycle
- Tumble Dry, Low Heat
- Tumble Dry, Low Heat, Permanent Press
- Tumble Dry, Low Heat, Gentle Cycle
- Tumble Dry, Medium Heat
- Tumble Dry, Medium Heat, Permanent Press
- Tumble Dry, Medium Heat, Gentle Cycle
- Tumble Dry, High
- Do Not Tumble Dry
- Line Dry
- Drip Dry
- Lay Flat

DRY CLEANING

- Dry Clean Only
- Do Not Dry Clean

Iron Shine and Spots

*W*hen you place an overly hot iron on an extra-delicate fabric, things can go wrong quickly. Here is how you can reverse the damage done when you end up with pressing shine and spots.

Pressing Shine

When you press some fabrics with an iron that is too hot, the iron leaves a shiny spot on the fabric. You can remove the shine by rubbing the spot with a bit of fine-grit sandpaper, 200 grit or finer (the higher the number the finer the grain). Use sparingly and gently, but it should make your material all the same texture again.

Pressing Spots

Irons that have been stored while filled with water will develop a buildup of minerals. When the iron gets hot and you start to steam your clothing, the minerals will discolor and spot your clothing. To remove the spots, immediately soak the item in water and rub the area with something abrasive like table salt or baking soda.

To fix the iron, empty out the water and fill the chamber with an equal mixture of distilled water and vinegar. Let the iron sit overnight. On high heat and steam, press a scrap piece of cloth or an old pair of jeans. This will loosen the sediment in the steam holes. Empty the steam chamber and let the heat evaporate any remaining water. To prevent buildup from happening, empty the water chamber before storing the iron.

PRESSING SHINE

Rub spot out with fine-grit sandpaper.

PRESSING SPOT

Stain Solutions

Stains are always a pain. You can mend around them and you can patch over them, but the best thing to do is remove them before they get embedded in the fibers. Do not rub any stain unless a stain removal product directs you to do so specifically. Rubbing can grind the stain deeper into the fabric's fibers, making it much more difficult to remove. Also, heat sets stains, so do not dry anything until you are confident you have removed the stain the best you can.

A great stain remover lives in your kitchen: vinegar. Spray a solution of one part vinegar and one part water onto the stained area until it is thoroughly soaked. Let it set for a half hour and then rinse the garment. Keep soaking the fabric with the vinegar and water solution and rinsing it until the stain is gone.

Kick Three Tough Stains in the Pants

Red wine: Pour salt onto the stain and let it sit until the crystals turn pink. Salt actually leaches the pigment right out of the garment. Then, soak the affected area for as long as possible in water with a dash of laundry detergent. Overnight is best. Wash as directed by the clothing label and you should be good to go.

Chewing gum: Freeze it. Literally put the whole thing into the freezer until the gum is hard. Pick the frozen glob of gum off the garment and it should not leave any stain behind. If you cannot put the whole garment into the freezer, place a bag of ice over the gum-infected area.

Tomato sauce: Dab away, don't rub, all the excess sauce. Rinse the item in cold water. Use a nonabrasive sponge and some dish soap to sop up and dab away the stain. Rinse again and wash as normal.

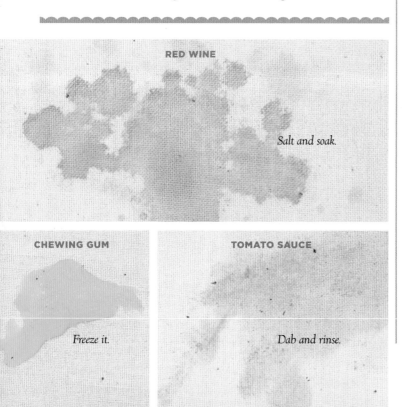

RED WINE
Salt and soak.

CHEWING GUM
Freeze it.

TOMATO SAUCE
Dab and rinse.

Megan Pederson developed this cute, quick fix to deal with her messy daughter's tendency to pick up stains on every new dress she wears. Megan applied double-sided fusible webbing to some fabulous fabrics, cut out a variety of shapes, and then adhered one to the dress wherever a spot or stain popped up.

Seasonal Storage

*I*t's important to *store and protect* your seasonal clothing safely. Make sure they are clean and dry before packing them up for the season. Avoid storing clothing in cardboard because it actually attracts insects. Large plastic storage containers and bags are a convenient storage solution if you don't have ideal storage space. Just be careful that your clothing is clean and completely dry before sealing it up. If there are any bits of food or moisture in the clothing, plastic storage containers can promote mold growth. If there are bug eggs in your clothes, any moisture in the containers will provide the nice humid atmosphere in which bugs thrive. Gross!

In and Out of Storage

•✦ Use white tissue paper to pad and protect clothing.

•✦ Use muslin to cover hanging items and layer between delicate items.

•✦ Moths are pretty pesky beasts, but unfortunately too many mothballs can be worse than the moths themselves. Cedar and lavender are natural moth repellents. If you do use mothballs, put them in an old sock or pillowcase so they don't touch any of your clothing directly.

•✦ Always completely clean and dry all items before storing them away. This definitely helps prevent against insects and mold.

•✦ To restore garments when they come out of storage, fluff them up in the dryer using the tumble dry setting or hang on the clothesline.

•✦ Knits, silks, and rayon fabrics should always be stored flat, to avoid stretching them out of shape.

•✦ Linen and metallic fabrics should be rolled to avoid creasing. Layer muslin fabric with each item before rolling to keep it well protected.

•✦ Leather, suede, and fur should be covered with muslin and stored hanging in a cool dark place.

SUITCASE MAKEOVER

Old, cleaned out suitcases and trunks make for the very best clothing storage containers, and what a fun use for those vintage suitcases. Just make sure to clean them out really well before using them for storage. Use spot upholstery cleaner to clean up any stains, spots, or other unknowns. To get rid of bad-news, suitcase smell, spritz it with 100-proof vodka and leave open in a well-ventilated area. In the case of my suitcase (pictured on page 192), it looked so bad, that I ripped out the liner completely, and used some extra-hot glue and quilted fabric to reline the whole thing.

MENDING AS DEVOTION

by Sherri Lynn Wood

I believe in creatively mending clothing because it connects me to a deeper desire to care for, repair, and tend to the worn-out places within myself and in my relationships with others. Mending for me is an act of devotion that nourishes my sense of personal agency, as conspicuously mended clothing can be a proclamation against consumerism.

Taking the time to mend often feels like a pause from the excitement of creating something completely new. Mending is slow work and the fix is impermanent. It's meticulous work, and can be tedious. What is the reward? I asked my boyfriend what he liked best about his mended jeans. "They're unique, and nobody has a pair like them," he replied. "I felt cared for, and my favorite pair of jeans was saved from oblivion."

Mending a hole or rip in a pair of jeans or a shirt is simple. Here are some simple steps.

What You'll Need

Item to be mended

Fabric scraps

#8 pearl cotton or embroidery floss

Mending supply kit (see page 24)

What You'll Do

Step 1. Begin by picking out a contrasting fabric to place beneath the hole, as an underpatch. I prefer a prewashed cotton, linen or, for something heavier, corduroy or denim. Stay away from wool or any material that will shrink or disintegrate with washing.

Step 2. Next, pick out contrasting thread. I prefer #8 pearl cotton, but embroidery floss will work just as well. With embroidery floss you can control the thickness of your stitch by splitting the floss into threads. Use two or three threads when mending something lightweight and five or six threads for jeans.

Step 3. Select a sharp embroidery needle. A thimble and embroidery hoop might be useful in some circumstances.

Step 4. Pin the underpatch, which should be bigger than the section being repaired, into place underneath the damaged area.

Step 5. Use a simple running stitch to encircle holes and rips. This will also secure the underpatch in place. I stitch about 1" from the edge of the damaged areas, sometimes doubling back and meandering around the area several times for aesthetic effect or to reinforce any weak material around the hole.

Step 6. Next use a blanket stitch to outline the hole, and to secure the edges of the damaged area to the underpatch. You can cut away frayed areas so that the underpatch shows through clearly, or you may choose to secure the frayed area to the underpatch with running stitches.

Step 7. Once you're finished with your stitching, turn to the back of the repair and trim the underpatch to ¼" from the outer edge of the running stitches. That's it! And there is always more to mend.

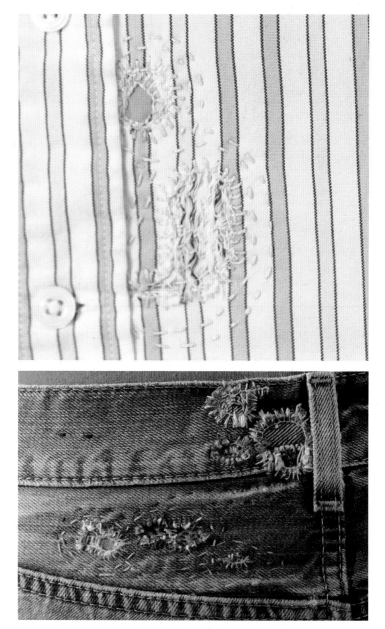

BLEACH-DYED SKIRT

by Rachel Beyer

When I was in high school, making a skirt out of an old pair of jeans was one of my first sewing projects. I think I originally read about the idea in a *Seventeen* magazine. Revisiting this concept 10 years later was a lot of fun and adding the bleach tie-dye really put the cherry on top of this simple project. It's a great way to "cover" a stain by completely removing any hint of it with bleach. It becomes a unique garment instead of a "don't mind that ink spot where my pen broke in my pocket."

What You'll Need

Old pair of jeans

Mending supply kit (see page 24)

Sewing machine (optional)

Bleach

Rubber bands

Plastic tub

What You'll Do

Step 1. Try on the jeans and use a chalk marker to mark a line just below the desired finished length of the skirt. Cut off one leg just above the chalk line. After cutting the first leg, fold the jeans in half and use the cut leg as a guide for cutting the remaining leg. Save the legs for patch fabric.

Step 2. Cut the jeans open along the crotch seam. Also, cut up about 2" on the center seam (toward the zipper).

Step 3. Next you'll want to create a clean triangular opening at the back of your jeans. If the jeans had worn holes in the thighs or along the crotch seam, cut off the worn areas. Using a ruler and chalk, draw a cutting line and then cut, as shown.

Step 4. Use the scrap fabric left over from the jean legs to cut out two triangles to fill in the crotch area. To determine the correct size and

STEP 2 *Cut the crotch seam.*

STEP 3 *Cut a triangular opening in the back crotch.*

shape triangles, lay the jeans flat with the back facing up and place your scrap piece in the crotch area. Make sure your fabric is smoothed out. Following the triangle shape of the crotch opening, draw a chalk line on the scrap fabric. Add ½" for seam allowance all around and cut the piece from the scrap fabric. Repeat step 3 and this step to measure and cut a second triangle for the front of the skirt.

Step 5. Lay the cut-up jeans on a table and for the front of the skirt, overlap the shaped and remaining part of the crotch seam (where you made that 2" cut) over the bottom layer, as illustrated. Pin the right side of the front triangle piece to the wrong side of the skirt front so it fills the opening. Do the same for the back of the skirt. It's fine if the triangle is longer at the bottom; you can trim that later.

Step 6. Topstitch along all the seams, by machine or by hand, removing the pins as you stitch.

Step 7. Trim away any excess fabric. You'll want to try the skirt on to make sure the bottom looks even. Trim a little more if necessary, but don't cut too much off, or your skirt will be too short!

Step 8. To dye the skirt, wet it (this makes it easier to fold) and bring the side seams together. Starting at one side, fold the skirt accordion style and secure the folds with rubber bands.

Step 9. Make a mixture of one part bleach and four parts water. Completely submerge the skirt in the solution. The longer you let it soak, the more dramatic your tie-dye result will be. I let mine soak for about 45 minutes.

Step 10. Once it's done soaking, rinse it in cold water and remove the rubber bands. Throw it in the washer with laundry detergent and then hang it to dry.

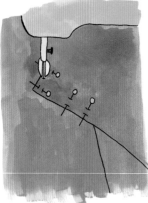

STEP 5 *Pin the triangle piece to fill opening on front.*

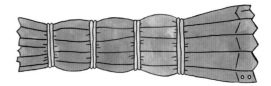

STEP 8 *Fold the skirt accordian style and secure with rubber bands.*

Resources, Glossary, and Contributors

Resources

BOOKS

Dupuy, Céline. *Simple Sewing with a French Twist.* Potter Craft, 2007.

Editors of Reader's Digest. *Complete Guide to Embroidery Stitches.* Reader's Digest Association, 2006.

Editors of Singer Worldwide. *Singer Simple Sewing Guide.* Creative Publishing International, 2007.

Editors of *Vogue Knitting* magazine. *Vogue Sewing.* Rev. ed. Sixth and Spring, 2006.

Gordon, Joan. *Stitch 'n' Fix: Essential Mending Know-How for Bachelors and Babes.* Guild of Master Craftsman, 2009.

Ides, Nan L. *Hand Mending Made Easy: Save Time and Money Repairing Your Own Clothes.* Palmer Pletsch, 2008.

Knight, Erika. *Simple Crochet.* Clarkson Potter, 2003.

Knight, Lorna. *The Sewing Stitch and Textile Bible.* Krause, 2007.

Singer, Ruth. *The Sewing Bible: A Modern Manual of Practical and Decorative Sewing Techniques.* Potter Craft, 2008.

Smith, Alison. *The Sewing Book.* DK Publishing, 2009.

Soule, Amanda Blake. *Handmade Home: Simple Ways to Repurose Old Materials into New Family Treasures.* Trumpeter, 2009.

ON THE WEB

BurdaStyle
www.burdastyle.com

Craft
http://craftzine.com

Craft Leftovers
www.craftleftovers.com

eBay
www.ebay.com

Etsy
www.etsy.com

Martha Stewart
www.marthastewart.com

Glossary

Animal Pelt. The skin of a furry animal; particularly referencing the skin after it has been removed from the animal's body.

Backstitch. In hand sewing, the backstitch is made by doubling back on itself (see page 50). In machine sewing, it is the reverse action that doubles back stitches and prevents them from coming unstitched.

Basting. The process of loosely sewing two or more pieces of fabric (or fabric and trim) to temporarily hold them together.

Basting Stitch. A long straight stitch on the machine or a long running stitch if working by hand.

Blanket Stitch. A buttonhole stitch that is spaced farther apart than usual and is used to reinforce the edge of material, such as a blanket, and keep the edge from fraying.

Blind Hem. A stitch that keeps the hem of a garment from unraveling, but isn't visible from the front. The blind hem also references a specific sewing machine stitch setting, which makes a blind hem stitch. See page 98 for how-to.

Blind Stitch. Also called the blind hem stitch, this stitch is worked by hand. Instructions for making a blind stitch are on page 99.

Buttonhole Stitch. Worked exactly the same as the blanket stitch, but with the stitches closer together. It is used in embroidery, tailoring, lace making, and of course making buttonholes.

Casing. A channel created in a garment to encase elastic.

Cure Time. The time it takes for a glue to reach maximum viscosity, which is a fancy way to say that the glue is all the way, completely, thoroughly dry.

Darning. The process of patching a hole by sewing a series of either woven stitches or knit stitches; see chapter 9 on darning techniques and inspirations.

Darning Egg. A very useful tool that helps create a work surface on which to darn; see page 126 for instructions on how to make your own.

Double Loop Knot. A sewing knot made by pulling the needle through a stitch's loop and then again through the resulting loop; see page 47 for instructions on how to make a double loop knot.

Double Overhand Knot. A variation of the overhand knot that is secure to the point of being difficult to take out. It is used to knot the end of a thread(s) so you can secure it to the fabric you are sewing (see page 47).

Embroidery Scissors. Small sharp scissors that are used in embroidery to trim threads closely to the back of work. They are sharp and great to use for snipping thread and fabric precisely.

Full-grain Leather. Leather that has not been altered other than the removal of the hair. It retains the original markings and texture of the hide.

Fusible Patch. Soft flexible fabric with one side coated in adhesive. Often the adhesive is heat activated, but it can also have a peel-off coating.

Fusible Webbing. A fiber that is man-made and will melt when heated (usually by an iron). It is not knitted or woven, but is instead a web of synthetic fibers. When you place the webbing between two pieces of fabric and heat them, it binds them together. Sometimes it comes with a paper backing, so you can fuse it to one layer at a time.

Grosgrain Ribbon. Tightly woven ribbon, identifiable by its ribbed texture.

Hem. The folded back and sewn edge of a garment. It can be used to form a finished edge or border an area.

Interfacing. A shaping material placed between layers of a garment to add body and stability. It is most commonly used in collars, cuffs, button bands, and pocket flaps. It can be used to give support and shape to not just garments, but also bags and other accessories.

Ladder Stitch. A stitch that invisibly closes gaps or creates a pronounced rib depending on the way it is stitched (see page 52).

Lapped. A kind of zipper; refers to the fabric that covers the zipper.

Lockstitch. The stitch made by a sewing machine. The top thread interlocks with the bobbin thread creating a stitch.

Multiharness Loom. A loom in which the warp threads are tied up to many lifting mechanisms, called harnesses. The harnesses are lifted in sequence to create a woven fabric.

Needle Board. A pressing tool used to help reset pile fabrics. It is a piece of leather or a thin board covered in many short needles.

Overcast. A stitch that is used to prevent unraveling (see page 48).

Patchwork. The process of piecing together fabric shapes to make a larger cloth.

Pile Fabric. A fabric with a surface composed of short upright yarns that are either cut or looped; read all about pile fabrics in chapter 12.

Pressing Cloth. A cloth used between a fashion fabric and the surface of the iron to prevent damage by scorching, burning, or flattening the fabric.

Prick Stitch. A stitch that is barely visible on the right side of the work (see page 50).

Reverse Appliqué. The process of cutting a shape out of an upper layer of fabric and stitching it to reveal the fabric below.

Running Stitch. Also referred to as the straight stitch, this stitch is worked by passing the needle in and out of the fabric at even intervals (see page 49).

Seam Allowance. The area between the stitching line and the cut edge of a piece of fabric.

Seam Ripper. A tool for removing stitches.

Seed Bead. A small, uniformly shaped bead with a general sphere shape. It is most commonly made from glass or glass substitutes and ranges in size from 1mm to 1cm.

Shank. In reference to buttons, the small knob on the back of a button with an opening for thread.

Suede Leather. The flesh side of the leather that has been finished with a soft, napped surface. It can also reference the outer side that has had the same treatment after the removal of a thin layer.

Tailor's Ham. A pressing tool used to press shaped seams and other shaped areas of a garment. See page 174 to learn how to make your own.

Thimble. A small cap worn over your finger or thumb to protect it from getting poked by needles. While traditionally made from metal or leather, they can now be found in plastic and rubber.

Twill Tape. Ribbon that is flat woven twill. It is especially strong and stretch-resistant.

Warp. The set of yarns that are placed lengthwise in a loom and are crossed by and interwoven with the **Weft** yarns, which are horizontally worked.

Zigzag Stitch. A back-and-forth stitch that is characterized by sharp angles and a zigzag pattern (see page 53).

Project Contributors

Susan Beal. "I'm a crafty girl with a lot of frequent flyer miles! I love to travel, and my husband, Andrew, and I split our time between Los Angeles and Portland, Oregon. I'm a freelance writer and nonstop crafter. I sell a line of handmade jewelry and A-line skirt kits under the name *susanstars*. I cowrote *Super Crafty* with the ladies of the Portland Super Crafty collective, and I've contributed how-to projects to a number of books. I also write for *Venus, Adorn, Craft, Cutting Edge, ReadyMade, BUST,* and GetCrafty.com. In my spare time, I love to sew dresses from vintage patterns, knit, embroider, make collages, hang out on flickr, read, drink coffee, and go to the Rose Bowl flea market! My big ambition is to make a crazy quilt with all my vintage fabric bits and scraps from projects past."
See page 80.
www.westcoastcrafty.com

Rachel Beyer is a native of Portland, Oregon. She received her BFA in graphic design in 2007 from the Art Institute of Seattle and has worked for various design companies in both the Portland and Seattle areas. Her love of crafts was originally inspired by her mother and grandmother, both of whom taught her to sew, crochet, and make jewelry at a very young age. In 2009, she started her own company, Camp Smartypants, selling handmade women's clothing and accessories inspired by her childhood memories of summer camp adventures. Today she works as both a freelance graphic designer and avid crafter in Portland.
See page 204.
www.campsmartypants.com
www.rachelbeyer.com

Deb Cory. Her business, Mama's Collection, is the culmination of sewing projects created from repurposed, collected items. Revitalizing old things into new, serving a new generation with collected vintage things, brings her great joy. Deb is old enough to remember the dawn of the word *ecology* and *recycle* in the '70s and is excited about the new movement of young crafters, eager to maintain sustainable resources. Deb has been married to the same tolerant man for 38 years, is a mother of four, mother-in-law to three, and grandma to two little girls. She has had the pleasure of knowing the author of this book since Kristin was six months old.
See pages 9 and 32.
http://sonowiknow.blogspot.com

Carina Envoldsen-Harris is a 30-something Dane living just outside London, England, with her English husband. She designs colorful, free-form embroidery designs under the name Polka & Bloom. Her grandmother (a crafty rock star) taught her to cross-stitch when she was very young

and Carina likes to think that Grandma would be happy to see her continue the crafty tradition. Carina writes a blog about her crafty adventures in embroidery, crochet, and sewing.
See page 71.
http://carinascraftblog.wardi.dk Embroidery designs on www.polkaandbloom.com.

Crispina ffrench. "A community activist, artist, mother, wife, and friend, my passions lie in environmental stewardship, alchemy initiation, and empowering people to be their best. In 1987, while at college, I started Crispina Designs, Inc. All the materials were from used clothing, production was domestic, and many of my employees worked at home. In 2008, I stopped running my wholesale company and transitioned into authoring my first book and teaching workshops to students from all over the country in my studio in Pittsfield, Massachusetts. Alchemy Initiative, an urban model of community and sustainability, began as an idea in January 2009 and by June of that year became a bona-fide five-person partnership. It has long been my preference to use what I have rather than to consume new things."
See page 78.
www.crispina.com

Jennifer Forest. With a professional background as a curator and teacher, Jennifer's love of history inspires her handmade crafts. Her passion for historical design and crafts led to her recent book, *Jane Austen's Sewing Box*. This book celebrates the Regency era with sewing, embroidery, knitting, and paper projects from that time. Each project includes quotes from Jane Austen's novels, historical notes, photographs, and instructions to make your own Regency projects. Jennifer has experience in a wide range of crafts but particularly enjoys working in sewing, embroidery, and felting.
See page 105.
www.sewing-box.net
www.jennifer-forest.com

Diane Gilleland is a writer and teacher who makes her home in Portland, Oregon. She also makes podcasts, videos, and blogs about crafting. She can always find a good excuse to craft instead of doing household chores.
See page 132.
www.craftypod.com

Pam Harris describes herself as a "happy dabbler" and her wide range of interests are reflected in her seasonally based crafty blog. Her favorite memories are of making stuff with her two children, now grown. While weaving, tin work, embroidery, gourd art, and wheat weaving have been the focus of her personal craft endeavors, she also enjoys quilting, paper craft, knitting, and felting. Pam and her husband are wedding and event photographers. When she isn't shooting or editing, Pam can be found in her kitchen or her garden.
See page 68.
www.gingerbreadsnowflakes.com

Marisa Lynch gave herself a yearlong challenge of spending 365 days creating 365 items of clothing on a 365-dollar budget. Her blog New Dress A Day is a chronicle of her yearlong journey that began when she got laid off from

her job and saw *Julie & Julia* the same weekend. Having a background in styling, fashion writing and editing as well as a penchant for quickly skimming through monthly issues of *Vogue* and *Lucky*, her fashion and sewing prowess truly came to fruition when the paychecks stopped coming in. Who says fashion can't be chic and fabulous for pennies? Definitely not Marisa.
See page 116.
www.newdressaday.com

Francesca Mueller. "I live with my husband and our three children in an ancient rural village in northern Italy, where we've learned about life in a small farming community, including hand crafts, gardening, self-reliance, and frugal living. My journey with my husband has covered a lot of road, from work in the city of London to months of backpacking throughout South America, to academic life in Rome where I became an anthropologist, to becoming parents in Milan, and now raising our three bilingual children in the country. On

my blog, Fuoriborgo, I capture some of this family journey."
See page 144.
www.fuoriborgo.com

Cal Patch has been a maker since she was a Girl Scout in the '70s. She sews, crochets, spins, embroiders, knits, prints, makes patterns, dyes — hence the name of her label: hodge podge. Cal has taught all of these subjects for the past 10 years, and loves showing people new skills. After 17 years of being a New York City dweller, Cal recently relocated to the Catskills where she plans to be a crafty farmer. Her first book, *Design-It-Yourself Clothes: Patternmaking Simplified*, is available from Potter Craft.
See page 128.
www.hodgepodgefarm.net

Stacie Wick. "I'm a crafting wife and mom and I teach my six kids at home. I am disorganized and a procrastinator, but I keep on trying to improve. Every day is an adventure."
See page 93.
http://stayseemakedo.typepad.com

Sherri Lynn Wood. Devoted with a rebellious heart, and with master's degrees in fine arts (sculpture) from Bard College and theological studies from Emory University, Sherri Lynn is an artist, quilt maker, and healer based in San Francisco. Sherri combines her interests in craft, sculpture, and human systems theory to reacquaint people with personal agency, community, love, and the basic skills of living. She has been making quilts since 1988.
See page 201.
www.daintytime.net

Additional Contributors of Inspirational Mending Ideas

Caitlin Stevens Andrews
See page 183.
http://stevenshandmade.blogspot.com

Maja Blomqvist
See page 165 and 186.
www.materialisterna.blogspot.com

Cathie Jo
See page 51.
www.bobetsy.etsy.com

Ágnes Palkó
See page 83.
www.worldaccordingtoagi.blogspot.com

Eirlys Penn
See page 26.
www.scrapiana.com

Megan Pederson
See page 199.
www.bridgetandlucy.com

Leah Peterson
See page 64.
www.leahpeah.com

Jamie Smith
See page 65.
www.creatingreallyawesomefreethings.com

Metric Conversions

STANDARD METRIC CONVERSION FORMULAS

yards × 0.9144 = meters (m)
yards × 91.44 = centimeters (cm)
inches × 2.54 = centimeters (cm)
inches × 25.4 = millimeters (mm)
inches × 0.0254 = meters (m)

STANDARD EQUIVALENTS

$\frac{1}{8}$ inch = 3.2 mm
$\frac{1}{4}$ inch = 6.35 mm
$\frac{3}{8}$ inch = 9.5 mm
$\frac{1}{2}$ inch = 1.27 cm
$\frac{5}{8}$ inch = 1.59 cm
$\frac{3}{4}$ inch = 1.91 cm
$\frac{7}{8}$ inch = 2.22 cm
1 inch = 2.54 cm

Index

Other Storey Titles You Will Enjoy

Fabric-by-Fabric One-Yard Wonders, by Rebecca Yaker and Patricia Hoskins.
101 more beautiful, stylish, and fun projects that use a diverse range of fabrics.
416 pages. Hardcover with concealed wire-o and patterns. ISBN 978-1-60342-586-5.

One-Yard Wonders, by Rebecca Yaker and Patricia Hoskins.
101 hip, contemporary projects, from baby items and plush toys to pet beds and stylish
bags, each made from just a single yard of fabric.
304 pages. Hardcover with concealed wire-o and patterns. ISBN 978-1-60342-449-3.

Sew & Stow, by Betty Oppenheimer.
Out with plastic bags and in with 30 practical and stylish totes of all types!
192 pages. Paper. ISBN 978-1-60342-027-3.

Sew What! Bags, by Lexie Barnes.
Totes, messenger bags, drawstring sacks, and handbags — 18 pattern-free projects that
can be customized into all shapes and sizes.
152 pages. Hardcover with concealed wire-o. ISBN 978-1-60342-092-1.

Sew What! Skirts, by Francesca DenHartog & Carole Ann Camp.
A fast, straightforward method of sewing a variety of inspired skirts that fit your body
perfectly, without relying on store-bought patterns.
128 pages. Hardcover with concealed wire-o. ISBN 978-1-58017-625-5.

The Sweater Chop Shop, by Crispina ffrench.
One-of-a-kind clothing and home dec items from recycled wool sweaters
176 pages. Paper. ISBN 978-1-60342-155-3.

These and other books from Storey Publishing are available
wherever quality books are sold or by calling 1-800-441-5700.
Visit us at *www.storey.com.*